more microwaving secrets

microwave cooking library®

by barbara methven

microwave cooking library®

No matter how familiar you are with microwave cooking, there's always something different to discover. To produce this book, a group of experienced microwave cooks explored new possibilities for using the microwave oven creatively.

In *More Microwaving Secrets* you'll find things that would be difficult — even impossible — to do without a microwave oven: virtually mess-free cooking with paper and plastic; natural containers as oven-to-table utensils; sinfully delicious confections made microwave-easy.

As you try the recipes, you'll learn new techniques as well as simplified microwave versions of familiar procedures. Even when you cook conventionally, many recipes have steps that can be done best in your microwave oven. No wonder microwave oven owners say, "I can't imagine how I ever got along without it."

Barbara Methven

Barbara Methven

CREDITS:
Design & Production: Cy DeCosse Incorporated
Senior Art Director: Bill Nelson
Art Director: Rebecca Gammelgaard
Managing Editor: Reneé Dignan
Associate Project Manager: Melissa Depew
Home Economists: Jill Crum, Peggy Ramette, Kathy Weber
Consultants: Joanne Crocker Prater, Carol Trench, Grace Wells
Recipe Editor: Bryan Trandem
Production Manager: Jim Bindas
Assistant Production Manager: Julie Churchill
Typesetting: Jennie Smith, Linda Schloegel
Production Staff: Janice Cauley, Joe Fahey, Carol Ann Kevan, Yelena Konrardy, Christi Maybee, Amy Peterson, David Schelitzche, Mary Vanpilsum, Greg Wallace, Nik Wogstad
Studio Manager: Cathleen Shannon
Photographers: Tony Kubat, John Lauenstein, Mark Macemon, Mette Nielsen, Rex Irman
Food Stylists: Sue Sinon, Melinda Hutchison, Lynn Bachman, Suzanne Finley, Robin Krause, Lynn Lohmann, Alicia Tessling, Susan Zechmann
Color Separations: Weston Engraving Co., Inc.
Printing: R. R. Donnelley & Sons (1087)

Additional volumes in the Microwave Cooking Library series are available from the publisher:

- Basic Microwaving
- Recipe Conversion for Microwave
- Microwaving Meats
- Microwave Baking & Desserts
- Microwaving Meals in 30 Minutes
- Microwaving on a Diet
- Microwaving Fruits & Vegetables
- Microwaving Convenience Foods
- Microwaving for Holidays & Parties
- Microwaving for One & Two
- The Microwave & Freezer
- 101 Microwaving Secrets
- Microwaving Light & Healthy
- Microwaving Poultry & Seafood
- Microwaving America's Favorites
- Microwaving Fast & Easy Main Dishes

CY DE COSSE INCORPORATED
Chairman: Cy DeCosse
President: James B. Maus
Executive Vice President: William B. Jones

Library of Congress Cataloging-in-Publication Data.

Methven, Barbara.
   More microwaving secrets

(Microwave cooking library)

Includes index.
1. Microwave Cookery. I. Title. II. Series.
TX832.M4157   1987   641.5'882   87-15450
ISBN 0-86573-552-2
ISBN 0-86573-553-0 (pbk.)

Published by Prentice Hall Press
A Division of Simon & Schuster, Inc., New York
ISBN 0-13-600867-4

Contents

What You Need to Know Before You Start

What is a microwave secret? It's something you can do faster, easier, better — or even exclusively — in a microwave oven. It's a new technique or a shortcut that takes a microwave advantage, like speed or easy cleanup, and makes it even better. A microwave oven helps you take a relaxed, playful approach to cooking, so the ultimate microwave secret is that microwaving can be fun and creative as well as fast and easy.

How to Use This Book

The first eight pages of this book present useful tips for easier microwaving. The chapters which follow suggest ways for using your microwave oven creatively. Read through the following short descriptions for ideas that appeal to you. Then turn to the recipes, tips and charts to share in the secrets.

Mess-free Microwaving

The easy-cleanup feature of microwave cooking can be even easier. A creative use of everyday household products like paper towels, plastic wrap or cooking bags improves microwave cooking while reducing cleanup. Turn paper towels, parchment or plastic wrap into utensils for the ultimate in mess-free cooking and throw-away cleanup.

Food-to-Go

Fast food from your microwave can be prepared quickly and eaten on the run either at home, like rolled cakes and sausage, or en route to work, school or play, like the 5-minute breakfast sandwich or carry-out burgers. Many offices, plants and schools provide microwave ovens in the lunchroom, so pack your brown bag with the makings of a delicious, hot, eat-in-hand lunch.

Nature's Own Containers

Enhance eye and appetite appeal by serving foods in natural bowls. With conventional cooking, time needed to heat fillings in the shell would soften and overheat the container. In the microwave, shells hold their shape and add flavor to fillings, which attract energy and heat through quickly. Edible or throw-away, natural containers eliminate cleanup.

Blue Ribbon Extras

You needn't search in gourmet food shops or county fairs to find specialty items that add subtle distinction to meals. Make the best from both worlds in your microwave. Colorful, freshly dried herbs, intriguing flavored butters, private-blend mustards and piquant pickles enhance your menus and your culinary reputation with a minimum of microwaving time.

Platter Presentations

Assemble, microwave and serve picture-pretty platters. As you prepare these appetizers, main dishes and desserts, you're also creating an attractive arrangement to present to guests. Hot foods go from microwave to table without delay for garnishing.

Sweet Shop

A microwave oven takes the fuss out of melting chocolate. You can even re-warm chocolate if it becomes too cool to work. Explore the candy-maker's art, from the children's favorite freezer pops, to confectioner's classics like truffles and pecan clusters, to spectacular candy pizzas.

A collection of special-occasion desserts employs microwave shortcuts instead of complicated, time-consuming conventional methods. The recipes illustrate useful microwave tips and techniques which you'll want to adopt in your day-to-day cooking.

Creative Crafts

A few minutes in the microwave oven speeds the drying process of fresh flowers and baker's clay. Create floral arrangements, wreaths and ornaments to decorate your home and give to friends.

In About 1 Minute...

Look at what you can microwave in a minute-plus. They're so easy, you'll hardly need any directions.

Scramble Eggs: Microwave 1 egg at High for 30 seconds to 1 minute, stirring once.

Heat Hot Chocolate: Microwave 1 cup at High for 1¼ to 2¼ minutes.

Heat Fudge Topping: Microwave ½ cup at High for 45 seconds to 1 minute.

Heat Frozen Burrito: Microwave 1 burrito (4 oz.) at High for 1 to 2½ minutes.

Reheat Pizza: Microwave 1 to 2 slices at High for 45 seconds to 1¾ minutes.

Reheat Burgers: Microwave 1 hamburger in bun at High for 45 seconds to 1½ minutes.

Heat Syrup: Microwave ½ cup at High for 30 seconds to 1 minute.

Heat Hot Dog: Microwave 1 hot dog in bun at High for 45 seconds to 1 minute.

Melt Cheese Dip: Microwave 1 cup at 50% (Medium) for 45 seconds to 1 minute, stirring once.

Soften Cream Cheese: Microwave 1 pkg. (8 oz.) at 50% (Medium) for 1½ to 3 minutes.

Defrost Orange Juice Concentrate: Microwave 1 can (12 oz.) at High for 1 to 2½ minutes.

Warm Up Fruit Pie: Microwave 1 slice at High for 45 seconds to 1 minute.

Combination Cooking Tips

Quick Broiler-browned Casseroles. Prepare gratins (crumb- or cheese-topped casseroles) in a broiler-safe dish or casserole. Microwave as directed, then place under broiler, 2 to 4 inches from heat, until browned, watching carefully. You can also use oven broiler for browning coffee cakes or crisps that use a brown sugar, crumb-type topping.

Fast Tortillas. Soften tortillas in vegetable oil on your conventional rangetop, according to package directions. Prepare filling and cook filled tortillas in your microwave for fast finishing.

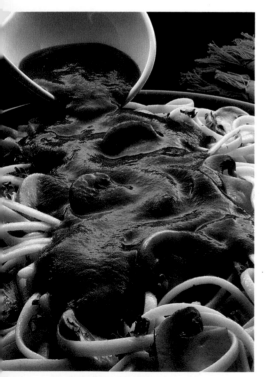

Quick Pasta Meals. Prepare pasta on your conventional rangetop while your favorite red or white sauce, meat or vegetable mixture is in the microwave.

Deliciously Browned Meats. For an attractive appearance, quickly brown pork chops or chicken pieces in a small amount of vegetable oil over medium-high heat on your conventional rangetop. Place meat on a roasting rack or in a casserole, and microwave to finish recipe.

Speed Grilling. Microwave chicken or ribs until almost done, then finish on the barbecue grill for a true charcoal flavor. Meat will be fully cooked and juicier with less chance of overbrowning. To give barbecued leftovers just-grilled flavor, reheat in the microwave.

Meringue Pies. Speed up preparation of meringue pies by cooking pie crust and filling in the microwave oven. Top with prepared meringue. Bake in preheated 400°F conventional oven until meringue is lightly browned.

Quick Ranch Fries. Extra baked potatoes from your microwave can be peeled and sliced into wedges, then browned in butter on your conventional rangetop.

Crispy Baked Potatoes. Partially cook whole potatoes in the microwave, then place in preheated 400°F conventional oven and bake until skins are dry and crispy.

Microwaving Tips

Clean up quickly. Use paper-towel-lined paper plates for microwaving canapés or nachos.

Line layer-cake dishes easily. Cut a circle of paper towel to fit bottom of 9-inch round cake dish. Paper absorbs excess moisture and provides smooth surface for frosting cakes.

Prevent spatters. Cover sauces that tend to spatter with a dry paper towel while they microwave. The paper towel allows steam to escape from spaghetti or barbecue sauces, and at the same time prevents spatters and absorbs excess moisture.

Absorb excess moisture. Place a paper towel under bread products and microwave just until warm. Towel will help keep bottom of bread dry.

Degrease soups and stews. Lightly place a paper towel on the surface of soups and stews after microwaving to absorb grease rising to the top during cooking.

Keep toppings crisp. Use paper towel as a cover when casseroles have crisp toppings. Towel holds in warmth while absorbing steam to prevent topping from becoming soggy.

Absorb grease. Layer 4 paper towels in bottom of 1-quart casserole. Crumble 1 lb. lean ground beef in casserole. Cover with another paper towel. Microwave at High for 4 to 7 minutes, or until beef is no longer pink, stirring once or twice to break apart. Remove top paper towel. Lift bottom paper towels, shaking ground beef into casserole. Use ground beef in tacos, spaghetti or other ground beef recipes.

Steam-heat dinner plates. Moisten 4 paper towels and place 1 towel on each of 4 microwave-safe plates. Stack plates and place in microwave oven. Microwave at High for 2 to 3 minutes, or until plates are hot. Remove from microwave using oven mitts.

Wax paper is an excellent cover for fruits or other foods that do not require steam to tenderize.

Catch drips by placing a sheet of wax paper under wire rack when cooling dipped chocolate candies.

Cover leftover foods with wax paper to hold in heat and moisture when reheating.

Line dishes with wax paper for easy removal of food. Cut wax paper to fit bottom of loaf and cake dishes — especially good for upside-down cakes and quick breads.

Spread candies, mints, drop candies or caramel corn on wax paper or parchment paper to cool after microwaving.

Hold in warmth by covering frozen foods with wax paper while defrosting in the microwave.

Use wax paper to cover custards and egg-based dishes. It holds in heat and promotes more even cooking. Because some steam escapes, surfaces will collect less moisture than when covered with plastic wrap.

Foil Tips

Shield wing tips and leg ends of whole poultry with small amounts of foil to protect them during defrosting and microwaving.

Keep bread products drier and crisper when reheating. Cut a piece of foil smaller than portion to be reheated. Place foil on plate in microwave. Cover with a folded paper towel. Place food on folded paper towel to reheat in microwave.

Wrap baked potatoes and tent whole roasts with foil during standing time to hold in heat and complete cooking.

Cover corners of square dishes and the ends of loaf dishes to help cakes, brownies, bars and quick breads cook more evenly during microwaving.

Use foil to shield and protect protruding angles and edges of roasts that may overcook because they are exposed to more microwave energy.

Microwaving with Foil:

- Keep all foil at least 1 inch from oven walls.
- Area of food exposed should be at least three times the area covered by foil (e.g., two-thirds of whole roast should be exposed).
- Crinkles in foil can sometimes cause arcing. Smooth out foil to fit close to food.
- Frozen convenience foods that come in foil containers should be transferred to a microwave-safe dish for more even defrosting or cooking.

NOTE: Always follow oven manufacturer's directions in regard to use of foil.

Protect thinner parts of foods — such as tails of whole fish, turkey tenderloin tips, thin ends of fish steaks — with small pieces of foil to prevent these areas from overcooking.

Mess-free Microwaving

Vegetables in Parchment

Microwaving with Paper Towels

Versatile paper towels absorb excess moisture from foods like bread or cookies, which need to stay dry. Towels prevent spatters and absorb fat and cooking juices so coated meats stay crisp. Dampened paper towels serve as utensils for cooking vegetables, chicken and seafood, while providing the moisture needed to steam them tender.

Drier baked potatoes. Scrub baking potatoes (8 to 10 oz. each) and pierce with a fork. Wrap each potato in a paper towel. Microwave until potatoes feel soft.

Amount	Microwave at High
1 potato	3 to 6 minutes
2 potatoes	5 to 10 minutes
4 potatoes	10 to 16 minutes

Let stand for 5 to 10 minutes.

Crisp, spatter-free bacon. Place bacon between layers of paper towels to absorb excess grease and prevent spattering. Cover bacon loosely with top paper towel to avoid sticking, and microwave until crisp.

Amount	Microwave at High
2 slices	1½ to 2½ minutes
4 slices	3 to 6 minutes
6 slices	4 to 7 minutes

Better vegetables. For brighter colors and better flavors, place 2 cups fresh cut-up vegetables (cauliflower, carrots, broccoli, green pepper or celery) on a plate and cover with a wet paper towel. Microwave at High for 2 to 3 minutes, or just until colors brighten. Rinse under cold water. Drain. Serve vegetables in dips, salads or as garnishes.

Seasoned Cocktail Toasts ▲

¼ cup butter or margarine
1 large clove garlic, cut into quarters
⅛ teaspoon onion powder
⅛ teaspoon seasoned salt
24 slices cocktail wheat or rye bread
Grated Parmesan cheese (optional)

2 dozen toasts

In small bowl, combine butter, garlic, onion powder and seasoned salt. Microwave at High for 1¼ to 1½ minutes, or until butter melts. Stir. Set aside.

Layer three paper towels on a paper plate. Arrange 8 slices cocktail bread around edge of plate. Brush tops of slices with small amount of melted butter mixture. Sprinkle with Parmesan cheese. Microwave at High for 1½ to 3 minutes, or until bread feels dry and firm, rotating plate once. Remove to cooling rack. (Bread crisps as it cools.) Repeat twice for remaining bread slices.

Cheddar-Bacon ▲ Bagel Chips

1 pkg. (6 oz.) bagel chips
1½ cups shredded Cheddar cheese
4 slices bacon, cooked crisp (page 16), crumbled

4 to 6 servings

Spread bagel chips evenly on two paper plates lined with paper towels. Sprinkle evenly with Cheddar cheese. Microwave each plate at High for 1 to 1½ minutes, or until cheese melts, rotating plate once. Sprinkle evenly with crumbled bacon.

Swiss Cheese Bagel Chips:
Follow recipe above; except substitute Swiss cheese for Cheddar cheese, and 1 tablespoon sliced almonds for the crumbled bacon.

Macaroon S'mores ▲

4 coconut macaroon cookies (2 to 2½-inch)
2 small squares of milk chocolate candy bar
2 large marshmallows

2 cookies

Fold a paper towel in quarters and place on a paper plate. Place 2 cookies on plate and top each with a chocolate square and a marshmallow. Microwave at High for 10 to 20 seconds, or until marshmallows puff. Top with remaining cookies.

Mexican Chicken Fingers

- ½ cup unseasoned dry bread crumbs
- ½ teaspoon paprika
- ¼ teaspoon garlic salt
- 1 egg
- 2 teaspoons lime juice
- 1½ teaspoons Mexican seasoning
- 1 lb. boneless whole chicken breasts, skin removed

4 to 6 servings

On paper towel or wax paper, mix bread crumbs, paprika and garlic salt. Set aside. In 9-inch pie plate, blend egg, lime juice and Mexican seasoning. Set aside.

Separate tenderloins from breasts to form "fingers." Form additional fingers by cutting remaining chicken breast meat into 1-inch strips.

Layer two paper towels on a plate. Dip chicken fingers in egg mixture, then roll in crumb mixture, pressing lightly to coat. Arrange fingers on plate. Cover with another paper towel. Microwave at High for 4 to 6 minutes, or until chicken is firm and cooked through, rotating plate once. Serve chicken fingers with salsa or taco sauce, sour cream or guacamole, if desired.

Spicy Bacon Snacks

Coating:

- ⅔ cup unseasoned dry bread crumbs
- 1 teaspoon chili powder
- ¾ teaspoon ground cumin
- ½ teaspoon cayenne

- 1 egg
- 2 tablespoons water
- 1 teaspoon white vinegar
- 6 slices bacon, cut in half crosswise

2 dozen snacks

Mix bread crumbs and spices on paper towel or wax paper. Set aside. In pie plate, blend egg, water and vinegar. Dip each bacon piece in egg mixture, then coat with crumb mixture.

Layer three paper towels on a 12-inch round platter. Arrange 6 bacon pieces on platter. Cover with another paper towel. Microwave at High for 2 to 4 minutes, or just until crisp, rotating platter once. Cut each bacon piece in half. Set aside. Repeat with remaining bacon. Serve warm.

Chicken Snacks ▲ with Honey Sauce

    2 tablespoons honey
 1½ teaspoons Dijon mustard
    1 teaspoon orange
        marmalade
    4 drops red pepper sauce
    6 oz. frozen breaded chicken
        chunks

1 to 2 servings

In small bowl, combine all ingredients, except chicken chunks. Mix well. Microwave at High for 15 to 30 seconds, or until mixture is warm and marmalade is melted. Set aside. Arrange chicken snacks in circle on paper-towel-lined plate. Cover with another paper towel. Microwave at High for 2½ to 4½ minutes, or until hot, rotating plate once or twice. Serve chicken chunks with sauce.

Cornbread-coated Cutlets

Coating:
 ¾ cup cornbread stuffing mix
    1 teaspoon dried parsley flakes
 ¼ teaspoon paprika
 ¼ teaspoon salt
 ⅛ teaspoon pepper

    1 egg
    1 tablespoon milk
 ½ lb. turkey cutlets (¼ inch thick)

Tangy Topping:
 ¼ cup sour cream
    2 tablespoons mayonnaise or
        salad dressing
    1 teaspoon dried parsley flakes
    1 teaspoon Dijon mustard

2 servings

Combine all coating ingredients in food processor or blender. Process into fine crumbs. Spread coating mixture on paper towel or wax paper. Set aside. In 9-inch pie plate, blend egg and milk. Dip cutlets in egg mixture, then roll in crumb mixture, pressing lightly to coat.

Layer two paper towels on a plate. Arrange cutlets on plate. Cover loosely with another paper towel. Microwave at 70% (Medium High) for 4½ to 8 minutes, or until turkey is firm and no longer pink, rotating plate once. Mix topping ingredients in small bowl. Serve cutlets with Tangy Topping. Serve as sandwiches, if desired.

Steamed Garden Vegetables

1 cup fresh broccoli flowerets
½ cup thinly sliced carrot
    Dash dried thyme leaves
¼ cup water
1 to 1½ teaspoons butter or
    margarine

                1 to 2 servings

Following directions (below), combine broccoli and carrots on one of two connected paper towels. Sprinkle vegetables with thyme. Close towels and moisten evenly with water. Microwave at High for 3 to 4½ minutes, or until vegetables are tender-crisp. Let stand for 2 minutes. Top with butter.

How to Microwave Food in Paper Towels

Leave two paper towels connected. Place one paper towel on plate. Place food in center of towel, then fold second towel at perforation, enclosing food.

Moisten paper towels evenly as directed in recipe. Fold in the unconnected sides to within 1 to 2 inches from food.

Microwave as directed. Let stand to complete cooking. Open carefully at perforation.

Szechwan Cauliflower

  2 teaspoons vegetable oil
 ½ teaspoon dried parsley flakes
 ¼ teaspoon sesame oil
    (optional)
 ⅛ teaspoon dried crushed red
    pepper
  1 cup small fresh cauliflowerets
 ¼ cup water

1 to 2 servings

In small mixing bowl, mix all ingredients, except cauliflower and water. Add cauliflower. Toss to coat. Following directions (opposite), place cauliflower on one of two connected paper towels. Close towels and moisten evenly with water. Microwave at High for 2½ to 4 minutes, or until cauliflower is tender-crisp. Let stand for 1 minute.

Lemony Asparagus ▲

  1 lb. fresh asparagus
  8 thin slices lemon, divided
  4 medium fresh mushrooms, cut
    into halves
  3 tablespoons chicken broth or
    water
  3 tablespoons white wine or
    water

4 servings

To clean asparagus: Gently bend spears until tough ends snap off. Discard end pieces. If desired, trim away scales from each stalk using a sharp knife.

Following directions (opposite), place 4 lemon slices on one of two connected paper towels. Arrange asparagus spears in thin layer over lemon slices. Top with remaining 4 lemon slices. Arrange mushroom halves around edges of asparagus. Close paper towels.

In 1-cup measure, mix chicken broth and white wine. Moisten paper towel packet evenly with liquid. Microwave at High for 7 to 10 minutes, or until asparagus stalks in center are tender-crisp, rotating plate once or twice. Let asparagus stand for 2 minutes before serving.

Basil-Orange Fish ◄

- 1 orange roughy fillet (4 oz.; about ½ inch thick)
- 1 green onion, thinly sliced
- 2 teaspoons snipped fresh parsley
- ½ teaspoon grated orange peel
- ⅛ teaspoon dried basil leaves
  Dash pepper
- ¼ cup water

Orange Sauce:
- 1 tablespoon butter or margarine
- 2 teaspoons orange marmalade
- ¼ teaspoon vinegar
  Dash salt
  Dash pepper

1 serving

Place fish fillet on one of two connected paper towels, as directed (page 20). Sprinkle with onion, parsley, orange peel, basil and pepper. Close paper towels and moisten evenly with water. Microwave at High for 2 to 3 minutes, or until fish feels firm and flakes easily with fork. Let stand for 2 minutes.

Combine sauce ingredients in small bowl. Microwave at High for 45 seconds to 1 minute, or until butter melts. Stir. Spoon Orange Sauce over fish fillet.

Wine-steamed Shrimp

- 3 thin slices lime or lemon
- ¼ lb. medium shrimp, shelled and deveined

¼ cup white wine

1 serving

Place lime slices on one of two connected paper towels, as directed (page 20). Top with shrimp. Close towels and moisten evenly with wine. Microwave at 70% (Medium High) for 2 to 4 minutes, or until shrimp feel firm. Let stand for 2 minutes. Serve hot with melted garlic butter, if desired.

Scallops Steamed in Broth: Follow recipe above, except substitute ¼ lb. bay scallops for shrimp, and ¼ cup ready-to-serve chicken broth for wine.

TIP: Steam small amounts of shelled and deveined shrimp or scallops in paper towels for quick main dishes, or to make ahead and refrigerate for seafood salads.

Chicken & Julienne Vegetables

⅓ cup julienne carrot
    (2 × ¼-inch strips)
⅓ cup julienne zucchini
    (2 × ¼-inch strips)
⅓ cup julienne yellow summer
    squash (2 × ¼-inch strips)
1 boneless whole chicken
    breast (10 to 12 oz.) cut in
    half, skin removed
    Lemon pepper seasoning
    Paprika
½ teaspoon dried parsley flakes
¼ cup water

Butter Sauce:

1 tablespoon butter or
    margarine
¼ teaspoon lemon juice
    Dash lemon pepper
    seasoning

1 to 2 servings

How to Microwave Chicken & Julienne Vegetables

Combine vegetables on one of two connected paper towels, as directed (page 20). Top with chicken breast halves. Sprinkle with lemon pepper and paprika.

Sprinkle parsley over chicken and vegetables. Close towels and moisten evenly with water. Microwave at High for 4 to 7 minutes, or until chicken feels firm, rotating plate once. Let stand for 3 minutes.

Combine sauce ingredients in 1-cup measure. Microwave at High for 45 seconds to 1 minute, or until butter melts. Spoon Butter Sauce over chicken and vegetables.

23

Microwaving in Parchment

Parchment packets steam fruits and vegetables in their own natural juices.

Vegetables in Parchment

1 parchment packet (below)
1 medium yellow summer squash, cut into julienne strips (2 × ½-inch)
½ cup diagonally sliced carrots (⅛-inch slices)
½ medium green or red pepper, cut into 1-inch chunks
⅛ teaspoon dried thyme leaves
⅛ teaspoon dried basil leaves
2 tablespoons butter or margarine, cut up

2 to 4 servings

In parchment packet, place squash, carrot and green pepper. Add remaining ingredients. Seal packet as directed. Place packet on 12-inch round platter. Microwave at High for 6 to 9 minutes, or until packet is very hot, rotating platter once. Let packet stand for 2 minutes before serving.

How to Form a Parchment Packet

Tear sheet of parchment at least 24 inches long. Fold in half. Place inverted 12-inch round platter on parchment, with edge overhanging folded edge of paper. Trace edge of platter on parchment.

Cut with scissors through both thicknesses of parchment, leaving circles attached at folded edge. Unfold to form one piece.

Place food in center of one circle. Close other circle over food.

Raspberry Fruit Compote

⅔ cup frozen unsweetened
   raspberries
3 tablespoons orange
   marmalade
   Dash ground nutmeg
   Dash ground cinnamon
1 medium apple, cored and
   sliced
1 small pear, cored and sliced
1 firm banana, cut into ½-inch
   slices
¼ cup slivered almonds
1 parchment packet (opposite)

4 to 6 servings

In medium mixing bowl, microwave raspberries at 50% (Medium)
for 1 to 2 minutes, or until defrosted.
Stir in marmalade, nutmeg and
cinnamon. Add remaining ingredients. Stir to coat. Place mixture
in parchment packet and seal as
directed. Place packet on 12-
inch round platter. Microwave at
High for 5 to 9 minutes, or until
packet is hot, rotating platter once.
Let packet stand for 2 minutes
before serving.

Roll and tuck edges of parchment, beginning at one side of
joined edge. Hold finger on last
fold while making the next fold.
Each new fold should seal
previous one.

Secure parchment packet by
folding end several times. Packet
should remain securely closed.

Open packet after microwaving
by cutting with scissors or unfold-
ing sealed edges. Open packet
carefully to avoid burns.

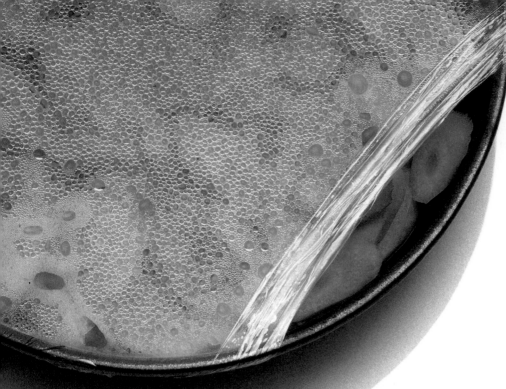

Microwaving with Plastic Wrap

Plastic wrap is a versatile kitchen aid that performs a variety of microwave functions. Use plastic wrap to hold in steam and speed cooking with dishes that do not have covers. Leave a slight opening at one corner of dish to vent steam. To drain fats or liquids, hold plastic wrap down in place using oven mitts, and tilt dish to drain through vent opening. AVOID BURNS: Always be careful when removing plastic wrap after microwaving.

Easily Remove Cabbage Leaves

Remove and discard core from one medium head cabbage. Rinse cabbage and shake off excess water. Wrap loosely in one or two sheets plastic wrap. Place wrapped cabbage seam-side-down on plate. Microwave at High for 5 to 8 minutes, or until leaves are pliable. Let stand for 5 minutes. Unwrap and rinse cabbage under cold running water to loosen leaves. Carefully remove outer leaves. Use outer leaves for stuffed cabbage. Inner cabbage can be used in other recipes.

Removing Skins from Peppers

Cut ¼-inch slice off top of medium pepper. Remove and discard inside seeds and membrane. Wrap loosely in plastic wrap and place pepper seam-side-down on plate. Microwave at High for 4 to 6 minutes, or until soft. Let stand for 3 to 5 minutes. Carefully unwrap pepper and place in a bowl of ice water until cool, about 5 minutes. Peel off skin, working in sections from top to bottom. Use a thin-bladed knife to help peel, if necessary.

TIP: Removing skins from green or red peppers before slicing or chopping for use in salads or sauces makes them sweeter tasting.

Steaming Vegetables in Plastic Wrap

Wrapping vegetables in plastic wrap before microwaving helps retain nutrients and just-picked flavors. Use chart below for reference in following recipes. Prepare accompanying sauces while vegetables stand after microwaving.

Vegetables	Amount	Microwave at High
Artichokes, fresh	2 medium	5½ to 8½ min.
	4 medium	9½ to 15 min.
Cauliflower, whole, fresh	1 medium	7½ to 14 min.
Corn-on-cob, fresh	2 ears	5 to 10 min.
	4 ears	8 to 16 min.
Potatoes, whole, new	1 lb.	4 to 8 min.
Squash, Acorn, fresh	1 whole	8½ to 11 min.

Corn-on-the-Cob

Remove husks from ears of corn. Rinse. Wrap each ear in plastic wrap. Microwave as directed in chart (left). Let stand for 5 minutes. Carefully unwrap. Serve with plain or flavored softened butter (page 82-83).

Artichokes

Trim stems from artichokes. Cut 1 inch off tops. Trim sharp ends from each leaf. Rinse artichokes and shake off excess water. Brush artichokes with lemon juice to prevent browning. Wrap each artichoke in plastic wrap. Microwave as directed in chart (above), rearranging once. Carefully unwrap artichokes and serve with Caper Butter, if desired.

Caper Butter

¼ cup butter or margarine
1 tablespoon capers, drained
  Dash pepper

¼ cup

In small bowl, combine butter, capers, and pepper. Microwave at High for 1¼ to 1½ minutes, or until butter melts. Serve butter with artichokes.

Steamed Cauliflower with Cheese Sauce

Microwave cauliflower as directed in chart (above). Let stand. Remove lid from 1 jar (5 oz.) sharp pasteurized process cheese spread. Place jar in microwave oven. Microwave at 50% (Medium) for 1 to 2 minutes, or until cheese melts. Stir cheese and pour over cauliflower. Sprinkle with bacon bits or fresh snipped parsley.

Steamed Acorn Squash

1 whole squash
½ cup applesauce
1 tablespoon packed brown
   sugar
⅛ teaspoon apple pie spice
   Dash salt

2 servings

Cut squash in half crosswise. Remove and discard seeds and fiber. Set squash halves on a large sheet of plastic wrap. (If necessary, cut a small slice from bottom of each half so that squash will sit upright.) Mix remaining ingredients in small bowl. Spoon evenly into centers of squash halves.

Bring corners of plastic wrap together above squash. Twist lightly to seal. Place on plate. Microwave at High as directed in chart (page 27), or until tender, rotating plate once or twice. Let squash stand for 3 minutes. Unwrap carefully.

Steamed New Potatoes

1 lb. new potatoes
¼ teaspoon dried rosemary
   leaves
⅓ cup butter or margarine
1 teaspoon lemon juice

6 to 8 servings

Trim ½-inch strip from around center of each potato. Place potatoes on a large sheet of plastic wrap. Sprinkle with rosemary. Bring long ends of plastic wrap together and fold over potatoes. Fold in sides to form loose packet. Place packet seam-side-up on plate. Microwave at High as directed in chart (page 27), or until potatoes are tender, rotating plate once. Let stand for 2 minutes.

Combine remaining ingredients in 1-cup measure. Microwave at High for 1½ to 1¾ minutes, or until butter melts. Serve lemon butter over potatoes.

Quick Steamed Vegetable Packets

Combine vegetables for any of the following recipes in center of a 15 × 12-inch sheet of plastic wrap. Sprinkle vegetables with water, as directed. Bring long ends of plastic wrap together over vegetables. Fold sides in to form loose packet. Place packet seam-side-up on plate. Microwave at High as directed, or until vegetables are tender-crisp. Let packet stand for 2 to 3 minutes. Unwrap carefully.

Fresh Peapod Medley ▲

On sheet of plastic wrap, combine 1 cup fresh peapods, ⅓ cup diagonally sliced celery (⅛ inch thick), and 1 tablespoon sliced pimiento. Sprinkle with 1 tablespoon water. Fold as directed. Microwave at High for 2 to 3 minutes.

Cauliflower & Carrots

On sheet of plastic wrap, combine 1 cup frozen cauliflowerets and ⅓ cup thinly sliced carrots. Sprinkle with 2 tablespoons water. Fold as directed. Microwave at High for 3 to 4½ minutes.

Green Beans & Shallots

On sheet of plastic wrap, combine 1 cup frozen green beans and 1 thinly sliced shallot. Sprinkle with 2 tablespoons water. Fold as directed. Microwave at High for 5 to 6 minutes.

Gourmet Stuffed Chicken Breasts

2 boneless whole chicken breasts (10 to 12 oz. each), skin removed
1 tablespoon chopped onion
1 teaspoon snipped fresh parsley
¼ teaspoon dried crushed sage leaves
¼ teaspoon salt
Dash ground nutmeg
⅓ cup whipping cream

Sauce:
1 tablespoon butter or margarine
1 tablespoon all-purpose flour
⅛ teaspoon salt
Dash ground nutmeg
½ cup ready-to-serve chicken broth
2 tablespoons whipping cream
1 tablespoon sliced almonds

2 servings

How to Microwave Gourmet Stuffed Chicken Breasts

Use sharp knife to cut along membrane while lifting and pulling tenderloin away from chicken breast. Cut tenderloin into 1-inch pieces.

Place tenderloin pieces, onion, parsley, sage, salt and nutmeg in a food processor or blender. Process until mixture is finely chopped. With machine running, add whipping cream. Process until mixture is smooth, stopping to scrape sides of container, if necessary. Set aside.

Pound each chicken breast to about ¼-inch thickness between sheets of plastic wrap to prevent spattering. Spread processed chicken mixture evenly down centers of chicken breasts.

30

Fold in sides of chicken breasts and roll up, enclosing filling. Wrap each chicken breast loosely in plastic wrap, leaving ends untucked. Place seam-side-down on plate. Microwave at 50% (Medium) for 11 to 16 minutes, or until internal temperature registers 170°F, rotating plate once. Set aside.

Place butter in 2-cup measure. Microwave at High for 45 seconds to 1 minute, or until melted. Stir in flour, salt and nutmeg. Blend in remaining sauce ingredients.

Microwave at High for 2¼ to 3 minutes, or until mixture thickens and bubbles, stirring twice. Carefully unwrap chicken breasts. Pour sauce over chicken and sprinkle with sliced almonds to serve.

31

Microwaving in Cooking Bags

Apricot-Pear Fruit Soup

2 pears, cored and sliced
1 pkg. (6 oz.) dried apricots
½ cup packed brown sugar
¼ cup currants
4 slices orange
3 tablespoons quick-cooking
  tapioca
1 cinnamon stick
¼ teaspoon anise
  seed, crushed
⅛ teaspoon salt
2½ cups water
½ cup port wine

6 to 8 servings

Marinate, cook and store in a single nylon cooking bag. Sturdy bags hold in steam to tenderize tougher cuts of meat. They also withstand time, heat and liquids necessary for tenderizing and rehydrating.

In nylon cooking bag, place all ingredients, except water and wine. Holding bag upright, add water and wine. Shake bag gently to mix. Secure bag loosely. Place bag in 9-inch square baking dish. Microwave at High for 5 minutes. Turn bag over. Microwave at 50% (Medium) for 14 to 24 minutes longer, or until fruit is tender and mixture is thickened, carefully turning bag once or twice. Let bag stand for 5 to 8 minutes before serving.

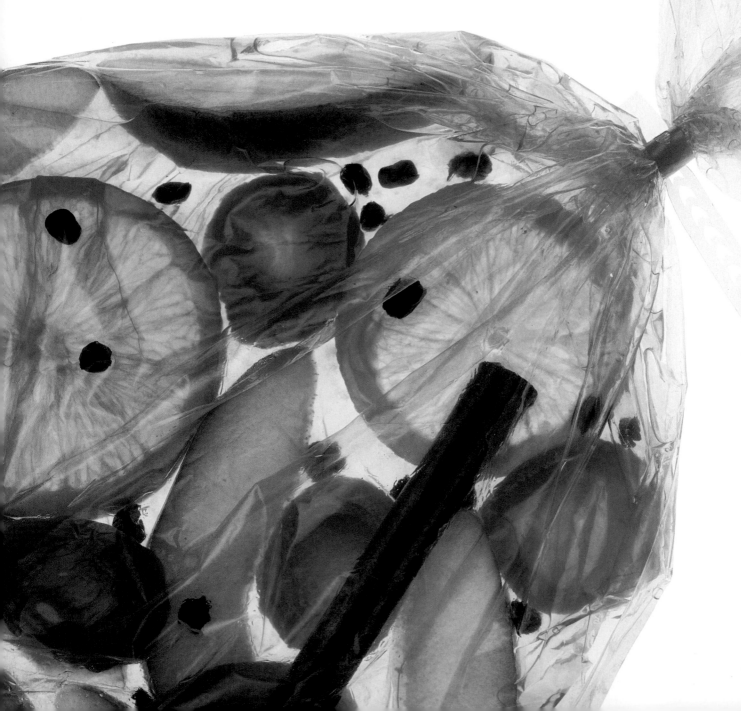

Cooking Bag Tips

Coat bag by placing 1 tablespoon flour in bag before microwaving. Shake to distribute flour, then proceed with recipe. Additional flour listed with ingredients is needed for thickening.

Secure bag loosely with nylon ties provided or string, to allow some steam to escape. DO NOT use metal twist ties: arcing may occur during microwaving.

Use oven mitts or pot holders when handling nylon cooking bags during or after microwaving. Bags retain heat from food.

Beef & Broccoli

½ cup water
⅓ cup sliced green onions
¼ cup soy sauce
3 tablespoons honey
1 tablespoon sherry
1 tablespoon all-purpose flour
¼ teaspoon grated fresh gingerroot
¼ teaspoon instant beef bouillon granules
⅛ teaspoon garlic powder
2 lbs. boneless beef top round steak (½ inch thick), thinly sliced
1 cup diagonally sliced carrots (¼-inch slices)
3 cups broccoli flowerets and thinly sliced stalks (about ¾ lb.)

6 servings

In nylon cooking bag, place water, onions, soy sauce, honey, sherry, flour, gingerroot, bouillon and garlic powder. Shake bag gently to mix. Add beef strips. Secure bag. Refrigerate for at least 4 hours. Place bag in 9-inch square baking dish. Add carrots to bag. Secure bag loosely. Microwave at High for 5 minutes. Microwave at 50% (Medium) for 30 to 40 minutes longer, or until meat is tender, adding broccoli during last 5 minutes. Let bag stand for 5 to 8 minutes before serving.

Fruited Wild Rice

¾ cup wild rice, rinsed and drained
½ cup chopped carrots
¼ cup uncooked brown rice
¼ cup raisins
¼ cup sliced green onions

2 tablespoons butter or margarine
½ teaspoon salt
¼ teaspoon ground coriander
2¼ cups water
½ cup apple juice

4 to 6 servings

In nylon cooking bag, combine all ingredients, except water and apple juice. Holding bag upright, add water and apple juice. Shake bag gently to mix. Secure bag loosely. Place bag in 9-inch square baking dish. Microwave at High for 5 minutes. Microwave at 50% (Medium) for 40 to 55 minutes longer, or until rice is tender and liquid is absorbed. Let bag stand for 5 to 8 minutes before serving.

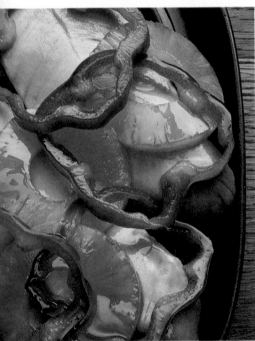

Turkey Hawaiian Style

¼ cup sherry
2 tablespoons soy sauce
1 tablespoon honey
¼ teaspoon ground ginger
¼ teaspoon salt
⅛ teaspoon pepper

2 turkey tenderloins (10 to 12 oz. each)
1 can (20 oz.) sliced pineapple, drained
1 green pepper, cored and sliced into ¼-inch rings

4 to 6 servings

In nylon cooking bag, place sherry, soy sauce, honey, ginger, salt and pepper. Knead bag gently to mix. Add tenderloins. Top with pineapple slices. Secure bag loosely. Place bag on plate. Microwave at High for 10 minutes. Add green pepper rings. Re-secure bag. Microwave at High for 3 to 8 minutes, or until turkey is firm and no longer pink, rotating plate once. Let bag stand for 5 minutes before serving.

Lamb & Lentil Stew

2 lbs. boneless lamb shoulder, cut into 1-inch cubes
2 cups uncooked lentils
1 can (16 oz.) stewed tomatoes
1 tablespoon all-purpose flour
1 teaspoon dried marjoram leaves

1 teaspoon sugar
¾ teaspoon salt
2 bay leaves
¼ teaspoon garlic powder
2 cups water
2 cups frozen cut green beans

6 to 8 servings

In nylon cooking bag, place all ingredients, except water and green beans. Holding bag upright, add water and knead bag gently to mix. Secure bag loosely. Place bag in 9-inch square baking dish. Microwave at High for 10 minutes. Microwave at 50% (Medium) for 30 minutes longer. Add green beans to bag. Re-secure bag. Microwave at 50% (Medium) for an additional 15 to 20 minutes, or until beans and lentils are tender. Remove bay leaves. Let bag stand for 5 minutes before serving.

Oriental Ribs ▲

½ cup hoisin sauce
¼ cup currant or plum jelly
1 teaspoon minced fresh
   gingerroot
½ teaspoon five-spice powder
3 lbs. pork spare ribs, cut into
   serving-size pieces

2 to 4 servings

In nylon cooking bag, place all ingredients, except ribs. Knead
bag gently to mix. Add ribs. Turn
bag over and knead gently to
coat ribs. Secure bag loosely.
Place bag on platter. Microwave
at High for 5 minutes. Microwave
at 50% (Medium) for 1¼ to 1½
hours longer, or until ribs are tender, carefully turning bag over
once or twice. Let bag stand for
5 to 10 minutes before serving.

Pork Roast with Red Cabbage

1 tablespoon all-purpose flour
1 teaspoon instant chicken
   bouillon granules
¼ teaspoon fennel seed,
   crushed
⅛ teaspoon mint flakes, crushed
1 medium onion, sliced

½ cup water
⅓ cup apple juice
¼ cup cider vinegar
2½ to 3-lb. boneless pork loin
   roast
1 medium head red cabbage
   (about 1½ lbs.) cut into 8
   wedges

6 to 8 servings

In nylon cooking bag, place flour, bouillon, fennel seed and mint flakes.
Add onion. Holding bag upright, pour in water, apple juice and vinegar.
Knead bag gently to mix. Add pork roast, turning bag gently to coat.
Secure bag loosely. Place bag in 9-inch square baking dish. Microwave
at High for 5 minutes. Microwave roast at 50% (Medium) for 40 to 50
minutes longer, or until internal temperature in several places reaches
165°F, carefully turning bag over once. Remove roast, reserving juices in
bag. Place roast on serving platter. Cover roast loosely with tented foil.
Set aside.

Add cabbage wedges to juices in cooking bag. Re-secure bag loosely.
Microwave at High for 6 to 9 minutes, or until cabbage is tender. Serve
cabbage and sauce with roast.

Hot Stuffed Polish Sausage

Microwave Lunches to Go

Small containers, plastic bags, foil and paper towels wrap things up for quick, on-site assembly. Before packing your lunch, toast breads, if needed, and divide fillings into single servings. Remember to refrigerate perishables until lunchtime. Assemble and heat as directed.

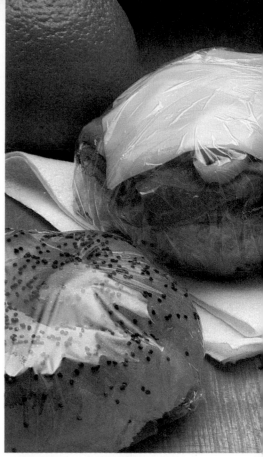

Stuffed Polish Sausage. Stuff sausage at home. Place in plastic container, plastic bag or foil. Wrap bun with plastic or foil to prevent drying. Take along packet of mustard, if desired. Pack paper towel.

Hot Pepper Deli Melt. Assemble sandwich and wrap in plastic or foil. Pack paper towel. To serve, remove overwrap and microwave open-face sandwich on paper towel.

Crab Rice Cake. Pack one serving crab filling in small container. Wrap rice cake in plastic wrap and cheese slice in plastic. Optional cucumber can be packed in sealable plastic bag.

Stuffed Pita Breads. Pack salad in plastic container. Wrap toppings together in plastic. Pack with salad. Wrap pita in plastic wrap or bag. Pack everything with cereal bowl in brown bag. Pack paper towel.

Egg and Ham-topped Bagel. Split and toast bagel; wrap in plastic or bag. Pack one serving of cheese-ham-egg filling in small container. Pack paper towel.

Baby Burgers

For each burger: Shape 2 oz. ground beef into round 3½-inch patty, about ¼ inch thick. Place on roasting rack. Microwave at High as directed in chart (below), or until meat is firm and no longer pink, rotating rack once. Cover with wax paper and let stand for 2 minutes. If desired, cut 1 slice (¾ oz.) pasteurized process cheese food into 4 squares. Place 1 square on each burger. Place burger in small bun (2½ to 3-inch diameter). Heat from burger will melt cheese.

Amount	Microwave at High
2 patties	1 to 2½ minutes
4 patties	2 to 3 minutes

Quick Burgers

For each burger: Shape 4 oz. ground beef into round 4-inch patty, about ½ inch thick. Place on roasting rack. Microwave at High as directed in chart (below), or until meat is firm and no longer pink, turning patties over and rotating rack once. Cover burgers with wax paper and let stand for 2 minutes.

Amount	Microwave at High
2 patties	2½ to 4½ minutes
4 patties	4½ to 7½ minutes

Prepare choice of Toppings (right), and spoon over cooked hamburger patties.

Barbecue Onion Burger Topping

1 medium onion, sliced ¼ inch thick
1 tablespoon barbecue sauce

Place onion in 1-quart casserole. Drizzle with barbecue sauce. Cover. Microwave at High for 3 to 4½ minutes, or until onion is tender-crisp, stirring once.

Italian Pepper Burger Topping

1 small green pepper, cut into ¼-inch strips
1 small red pepper, cut into ¼-inch strips
2 tablespoons olive oil
¼ teaspoon Italian seasoning

In 1-quart casserole, place green and red pepper strips. Drizzle with oil. Sprinkle with Italian seasoning. Cover. Microwave at High for 4 to 5½ minutes, or until peppers are tender-crisp, stirring once.

40

Hot Pepper Deli Melt ▲

For each sandwich: Sprinkle small amount of Italian dressing on bottom half of 4-inch French roll or Kaiser roll. Top with 1 to 2 oz. thinly sliced fully cooked ham, turkey or beef. Add fresh onion ring slices and mushroom slices. Sprinkle with hot pickled pepper rings. Top with one slice (¾ oz.) mozzarella or Colby cheese. Fold paper towel in quarters. Place open-face sandwich on towel in microwave oven. Microwave at High for 30 seconds to 1 minute, or until cheese melts. Add top half of roll to serve. For 2 sandwiches, microwave at High for 1 to 1¾ minutes.

Pork Applesauce Sandwich

For each sandwich:
1 thin slice cooked pork roast
1 English muffin half, toasted
1 to 2 teaspoons applesauce
1 tablespoon shredded
   Cheddar cheese

Place pork slice on toasted muffin half. Spread with applesauce. Sprinkle with cheese. Fold paper towel in quarters. Place sandwich on towel in microwave oven. Microwave at High as directed (below), or until cheese melts.

Amount	Microwave at High
1 sandwich	30 to 45 seconds
2 sandwiches	¾ to 1½ minutes

Hot Stuffed Polish Sausages in Buns

Slit fully cooked Polish sausages lengthwise, starting ½ inch from ends, being careful not to cut all the way through. Fill sausages with 2 teaspoons pickle relish or chopped onion, or with thin strip of cheese. Place sausage in bun and wrap in paper towel. Microwave at High as directed in chart (right), or until heated through.

Amount	Microwave at High
1 sausage	¾ to 1¼ minutes
2 sausages	1¼ to 1¾ minutes

Vegie Bagels ▲

Bagel halves, toasted
Lemon-Basil Cream Cheese
  (page 85)

Toppings:
Chopped fresh tomatoes
Chopped green pepper
Sliced green onions
Sliced olives (pimiento-stuffed
  or pitted black)

Spread toasted bagel halves
with Lemon-Basil Cream Cheese.
Top with one or more toppings,
as desired. Store any remaining
Lemon-Basil Cream Cheese in refrigerator no longer than 2 weeks.

Mexican Pizza Muffins ▲

1 English muffin, split and
  toasted
  Taco sauce
2 slices salami
  Chopped green chilies

Sliced black olives
Sliced green onion
2 tablespoons shredded
  Monterey Jack cheese

1 serving

Spread toasted muffin halves lightly with sauce. Top each half with 1 slice
salami. Sprinkle muffin halves with chilies, olives and onion. Sprinkle
evenly with cheese. Place muffins on paper-towel-lined plate. Microwave at High for 30 seconds to 1 minute, or until cheese melts, rotating
plate once.

For two servings: Double all ingredients. Prepare 4 muffin halves as
directed above. Microwave at High for 1 to 2 minutes.

Quick Pizza Muffins ▲

1 English muffin, split and
   toasted
   Pizza sauce
2 slices Canadian bacon
   Chopped onion
   Chopped mushrooms
2 tablespoons shredded
   mozzarella cheese

1 serving

Spread toasted muffin halves lightly with sauce. Top each half with 1 slice Canadian bacon. Sprinkle muffin halves with onion and mushrooms. Sprinkle evenly with cheese. Place muffins on paper-towel-lined plate. Microwave at High for 30 seconds to 1 minute, or until cheese melts, rotating plate once.

Egg & Ham-topped Bagels ▲

1 pkg. (3 oz.) cream cheese
½ cup chopped fully cooked
   ham
2 hard-cooked eggs, chopped
2 tablespoons sliced green
   onion

2 tablespoons finely shredded
   Swiss cheese
1 tablespoon mustard-
   mayonnaise sandwich sauce
   Toasted bagel halves

1¼ cups filling

In small bowl, microwave cream cheese at High for 15 to 30 seconds, or until softened. Add remaining ingredients, except bagels. Blend well. Spread 3 to 4 tablespoons ham mixture on one toasted bagel half. Fold paper towel in quarters. Place bagel half on towel in microwave oven. Microwave at High for 20 to 40 seconds, or until heated through. Repeat with additional bagel halves, or refrigerate ham mixture for later use.

For two bagel halves: Microwave at High for 30 to 50 seconds.

Stuffed Pita Breads

For each sandwich:
⅓ cup prepared chicken or tuna
  salad
½ loaf pita bread (6-inch loaf)
2 teaspoons sweet pickle relish
  or sliced green onion
  Chopped hard-cooked egg
  (optional)
1 tablespoon shredded
  Cheddar cheese

Spoon salad into pita bread half. Top with pickle relish and chopped egg. Sprinkle with Cheddar cheese. Line small, shallow cereal bowl with paper towel. Place sandwich upright in bowl. Microwave at 50% (Medium) as directed in chart (below), or until sandwich is heated through and cheese is melted.

Amount	Microwave at High
1 pita half	1½ to 3 minutes
2 pita halves	2 to 3 minutes

Chicken-Broccoli Tostadas ▲

½ cup frozen chopped broccoli
1 can (5 oz.) chunk chicken
⅓ cup shredded Monterey Jack
  cheese
¼ cup small-curd cottage
  cheese
8 to 10 drops red pepper sauce
4 tostada shells

4 servings

In small mixing bowl, microwave broccoli at High for 1 to 1½ minutes, or until hot. Drain. Add remaining ingredients, except tostada shells. Mix well. Spread chicken mixture evenly on tostada shells. Place tostadas on paper-towel-lined platter. Microwave at 70% (Medium High) for 2 to 3 minutes, or until cheese melts, rotating platter once.

Mexican Tostada ▶

For each tostada:

¼ cup refried beans
1 tostada shell
1 tablespoon finely chopped onion
1 tablespoon finely chopped green pepper
1 tablespoon chopped green chilies
2 tablespoons shredded taco-flavored Cheddar cheese
Taco sauce

Spread refried beans on a tostada. Sprinkle with onion, green pepper and green chilies. Top with Cheddar cheese. Place tostada on paper-towel-lined plate. Microwave at High for 1 to 1¾ minutes, or until cheese melts. Top with taco sauce.

Chicken & Pepper Tacos

¼ cup chopped onion
¼ cup chopped green pepper
¼ cup chopped red pepper
½ teaspoon Mexican seasoning
1 teaspoon vegetable oil
1 cup cut-up cooked chicken
½ cup shredded Monterey Jack cheese
⅓ cup ricotta cheese
¼ teaspoon salt
4 taco shells

4 servings

In small mixing bowl, combine onion, green and red pepper, Mexican seasoning and oil. Microwave at High for 2 to 3 minutes, or until vegetables are tender, stirring once. Mix in chicken, cheeses and salt. Spoon chicken mixture evenly into taco shells. Place upright in paper-towel-lined 9-inch square baking dish. Microwave at High for 1½ to 2½ minutes, or until mixture is heated through and cheese is melted, rotating dish once. Top with taco sauce or guacamole, if desired.

◀ Chili & Corn Tortillas

4 corn tortillas (6 to 8-inch)
1 can (15 oz.) chili beans in chili
   sauce, drained
2 tablespoons chopped onion
2 tablespoons chopped green
   chilies, drained
½ cup shredded Monterey Jack
   cheese
½ cup shredded Cheddar
   cheese

4 servings

Soften tortillas conventionally, as directed on package. Spoon beans evenly down centers of tortillas. Sprinkle evenly with remaining ingredients. Roll tortillas up, enclosing filling. Secure with wooden picks. Place tortillas on plate. Microwave at 70% (Medium High) for 3½ to 5 minutes, or until cheese melts, rotating plate once. Top with salsa or sour cream, if desired.

Biscuit Stackers

1 teaspoon mustard-mayonnaise
   sandwich sauce
2 baking powder biscuits, split
2 slices bacon, cooked (page 16)
1 slice (¾ oz.) pasteurized
   process Swiss cheese food

2 sandwiches

Spread sandwich sauce evenly on bottom halves of biscuits. Cut bacon and cheese to fit biscuits. Layer bacon and cheese over sauce. Add tops of biscuits. Wrap both sandwiches in paper towel. Microwave at High for 20 to 35 seconds, or until biscuits are warm and cheese is melted.

Variation:
Follow recipe above, except substitute 1 slice (1 oz.) boiled ham for the bacon, and 1 slice pasteurized process Monterey Jack cheese food for the Swiss cheese.

Five-minute Hot Breakfast Sandwich ▲

For each sandwich: Toast 2 slices bread or English muffin halves. Set aside. In small bowl, beat 1 egg. Microwave egg at High for 30 seconds to 1 minute, or just until soft-set, stirring once. Top one toast slice with 1 slice luncheon meat. Spread with scrambled egg. Top with 1 slice (¾ oz.) pasteurized process American cheese spread.

Fold paper towel in quarters. Place open-face sandwich on towel in microwave oven. Microwave at High for 30 to 45 seconds, or until cheese melts. Top sandwich with remaining toast slice.

Quick 'Cakes & Sausage

Place 2 fully cooked sausage links in center of paper-towel-lined plate. Place frozen pancake next to each sausage. Microwave at High for 1¼ to 2 minutes, or until pancakes are hot. Spread pancakes with favorite jam or maple syrup. Sausage can be rolled up inside pancake, if desired.

Blueberry Sauce ▲

1 tablespoon sugar
2 teaspoons cornstarch
  Dash ground nutmeg

2 cups frozen blueberries
2 tablespoons grape jelly

1¼ cups sauce

In 1-quart casserole, mix sugar, cornstarch and nutmeg. Add the frozen blueberries and jelly. Microwave at High for 6 to 8 minutes, or until mixture is thickened and translucent, stirring 2 or 3 times. Spoon sauce over waffles, pancakes or rice cakes.

Raspberry Sauce: Follow recipe above, except substitute 2 cups frozen raspberries for the blueberries.

◄ Apricot Topper

In small mixing bowl, combine ¼ cup orange marmalade, 2 tablespoons pineapple preserves, ¼ cup flaked coconut, 3 tablespoons chopped dried apricots, ⅛ teaspoon ground ginger and a dash salt. Mix well. Microwave at High for 1 to 1½ minutes, or until mixture is hot. Spread Apricot Topper on waffles, rice cakes, or pancakes.

Scotch-Mallow Snack ►

Spread marshmallow crème evenly on 1 whole graham cracker. Top with 1 tablespoon butterscotch chips. Fold paper towel in quarters. Place cracker on towel in microwave oven. Microwave at High for 20 to 25 seconds, or until creme puffs evenly. Heat will melt chips. Spread smooth with knife, if desired.

◄ Choco-Nut Bread

Spread peanut butter lightly on 1 slice banana bread (½-inch slice). Top with 1 tablespoon semisweet chocolate chips. Fold paper towel in quarters. Place bread on towel in microwave oven. Microwave at High for 30 to 45 seconds, or until bread is warm. Heat will melt chocolate chips. Spread chips smooth with knife.

Chocolate-Strawberry ◄ Rice Cakes

Top 4 rice cakes with thinly sliced fresh strawberries. Set aside. In 1-cup measure, combine ¼ cup semisweet chocolate chips, 2 teaspoons milk, 1 teaspoon orange-flavored liqueur and 1 teaspoon butter or margarine. Microwave at High for 20 seconds to 1 minute, or until chocolate can be stirred smooth. Drizzle chocolate sauce over strawberry-topped rice cakes.

Crab Rice Cakes ►

1 can (6 oz.) crab meat, rinsed, drained and cartilage removed	⅛ teaspoon garlic salt Dash pepper
¼ cup chopped green pepper	4 rice cakes
¼ cup mayonnaise or salad dressing	4 slices (¾ oz. each) Colby cheese
1 tablespoon sliced green onion	Cucumber slices (optional)

4 servings

In small mixing bowl, combine crab meat, green pepper, mayonnaise, green onion, garlic salt and pepper. Mix well. Spoon mixture evenly onto rice cakes. Top each with 1 slice cheese. Arrange cakes on paper-towel-lined plate. Microwave at High for 1¼ to 2 minutes, or until cheese melts, rotating plate once. Top each cake with cucumber.

Shrimp Rice Cakes: Follow recipe above, except substitute 1 can (4¼ oz.) medium shrimp, rinsed and drained, for the crab meat.

Cream Cheese ◄ Rice Cakes

Prepare one recipe Strawberry Cream Cheese, as directed (page 85). Spread rice cakes generously with Strawberry Cream Cheese. Refrigerate any remaining cream cheese. Top cakes with canned Mandarin orange segments, drained.

Nature's Own Containers

Creamy Squash & Apple Soup

Nature's Own Containers

You don't need an extensive collection of serving dishes or elaborate garnishes to present food attractively. Natural containers are fun, fancy and fuss-free. Microwaving heats fillings through without overcooking the natural shell.

Dress up plain foods with natural containers. An orange shell forms an individual dish for mashed sweet potatoes, while a large, glossy pepper holds cheese dip.

Wrap flavorful mixtures of meat and vegetables in edible leaves for satisfying main dishes.

Choose edible containers, like pepper or fennel wedges and onion shells to double as food and dish for a party meal.

Serve with style in natural bowls, like pineapple, eggplant or cabbage shells, for a dramatic presentation on a party buffet, or to add festivity to a family meal.

Fill natural cups, like mushrooms and cucumber chunks, with a savory stuffing to make elegant finger food for an appetizer tray.

Sausage-stuffed Mushrooms ▲

12 large fresh mushrooms
    (2 to 2½-inch)
¼ lb. bulk pork sausage
1 teaspoon instant minced
    onion

1 teaspoon dried parsley flakes
2 tablespoons seasoned dry
    bread crumbs
1 tablespoon grated Parmesan
    cheese

4 to 6 servings

Trim small portion of stem from each mushroom. Wipe caps clean with damp paper towel. Remove stems. Set caps aside. Finely chop enough stems to equal ¼ cup. Place chopped stems in 1-quart casserole. Discard remaining stems, or save for later use. Crumble sausage over chopped mushrooms. Sprinkle with onion and parsley. Cover. Microwave at High for 1½ to 2½ minutes, or until sausage is no longer pink, stirring once to break apart. Mix in remaining ingredients.

Stuff sausage mixture evenly into mushroom caps. Arrange stuffed mushrooms on paper-towel-lined plate. Microwave at High for 3 to 6 minutes, or until mushrooms are hot, rotating plate once.

◄ Corn with Lemon-Chive Butter

Prepare one recipe Lemon-Chive Butter (page 83). Set aside. Arrange 4 medium ears corn, in husks, in microwave oven. Microwave at High for 10 to 17 minutes, or until tender, rearranging ears once. Let corn stand for 2 minutes. Using oven mitt, hold each ear with tip pointing down. Pull back all but last layer of husk. Holding base of corn with mitt, grasp silk and pull sharply to remove. Remove remaining husk. Serve with Lemon-Chive Butter.

Stuffed Cherry Tomatoes ▲

1 pint cherry tomatoes
1 jar (5 oz.) blue cheese and
    cream cheese spread
⅓ cup shredded Cheddar
    cheese
4 slices bacon, cooked crisp
    (page 11), crumbled
2 teaspoons snipped fresh
    parsley
¼ teaspoon onion powder

6 to 8 servings

Cut thin slice from stem end of each tomato. With small spoon or melon baller, scoop out pulp. Discard pulp and tops of tomatoes. Place tomatoes cut-sides-down on paper towel to drain.

Combine remaining ingredients in small mixing bowl. Mix well. Stuff tomatoes with cheese mixture. Arrange tomatoes on paper-towel-lined plate, with smaller tomatoes in center. Microwave at High for 1½ to 2½ minutes, or until mixture is hot, rotating plate once. Sprinkle tomatoes lightly with snipped fresh parsley, if desired.

Savory Pepper Wedges

1 tablespoon plus 1 teaspoon
    butter or margarine
1½ cups cooked rice
  ½ cup grated carrot
  ¼ cup finely chopped zucchini
  ¼ teaspoon dried thyme leaves
  ¼ teaspoon salt
    Dash pepper
  1 medium red pepper
  1 medium yellow pepper

4 servings

In small mixing bowl, microwave butter at High for 45 seconds to 1 minute, or until melted. Add remaining ingredients, except red and yellow peppers. Set aside.

Remove and discard core and seeds. Cut each pepper lengthwise into quarters and fill pepper quarters evenly with rice mixture.

Arrange pepper wedges on plate. Cover with wax paper. Microwave at High for 5 to 7 minutes, or until rice mixture is hot and peppers are tender-crisp, rotating plate once. If desired, top peppers with snipped fresh parsley to serve.

Cheese Dip in Pepper ▲

In small mixing bowl, microwave 1 pkg. (3 oz.) cream cheese at High for 15 to 30 seconds, or until softened. Add ⅓ cup pasteurized process cheese spread and 2 tablespoons sliced green onion. Mix well and set aside.

Cut thin slice from top of large pepper (red, green or yellow). Set top aside. Remove and discard core and seeds. Spoon cheese mixture into pepper. Place pepper in a 6-oz. custard cup. Microwave at 70% (Medium High) for 2½ to 4 minutes, or until pepper is warm and cheese mixture is melted, rotating 2 or 3 times. Stir cheese. If desired, place pepper in center of raw vegetable platter to serve. Replace top of pepper, if desired.

Crab & Avocado Dip

1 large ripe avocado
  Lemon juice
1 pkg. (3 oz.) cream cheese
1 tablespoon sliced green onion
1 small clove garlic, minced
1 can (2 oz.) crab meat, rinsed,
  drained and cartilage
  removed; or ½ cup shredded
  seafood sticks
1 teaspoon lime juice
¼ teaspoon Worcestershire
  sauce
  Dash cayenne

6 to 8 servings

Cut avocado in half lengthwise and remove pit. With small spoon, scoop out pulp, leaving ¼-inch shell. Chop avocado pulp and set aside. Brush surfaces of avocado shells with lemon juice. Set aside.

In small mixing bowl, place cream cheese, green onion and garlic. Microwave at High for 15 to 30 seconds, or until cheese softens. Mix in chopped avocado pulp and remaining ingredients. Stuff crab mixture evenly into avocado shells. Place one shell on plate. Microwave at High for 30 seconds to 1 minute, or until dip is warm. Repeat with second avocado shell if needed. Serve dip with corn or tortilla chips, or assorted crackers.

TIP: Dip is conveniently served in its own natural container. Microwave one avocado shell, and refrigerate second shell until more warm dip is needed.

Date-Nut Apples

4 large cooking apples (8 to 10 oz. each)
2 tablespoons butter or margarine
¼ cup chopped pitted dates
2 tablespoons chopped walnuts
1 tablespoon maple syrup
½ teaspoon ground cinnamon

4 servings

TIP: Place cored apples in lemon-water to prevent browning. Combine 1 cup water with 2 tablespoons lemon juice in small mixing bowl. Dip apples in mixture and shake off excess.

How to Microwave Date-Nut Apples

Core apples, leaving ½ inch attached at bottom. With thin, flexible knife, make curved, diagonal cuts, starting at top. Cuts should be 1½ inches long and about ½ inch apart. Place in 9-inch round cake dish. Set aside.

Place butter in small mixing bowl. Microwave at High for 45 seconds to 1 minute, or until melted. Add dates, walnuts, maple syrup and cinnamon. Mix well.

Spoon mixture evenly into apples. Cover with plastic wrap. Microwave at High for 8 to 11 minutes, or until apples are tender, rotating and rearranging once. Serve in individual dishes. Spoon any cooking liquid over apples.

Ricotta Fruit-filled Pears

¾ cup sugar
½ cup water
2 teaspoons lemon juice
2 large pears (8 to 10 oz. each)
½ cup ricotta cheese
1 tablespoon sugar
1 teaspoon vanilla
¼ cup diced dried mixed fruits
¼ cup chopped candied
   cherries

4 servings

In medium mixing bowl, combine sugar, water and lemon juice. Mix well. Microwave at High for 3 to 4½ minutes, or until mixture boils. Stir until sugar dissolves. Set aside. Core pears and peel. Cut each pear in half lengthwise. Using melon baller, scoop out slight hollow for filling. Place halves in syrup mixture. Cover with plastic wrap. Microwave pears at High for 4 to 8 minutes, or until translucent and tender, rearranging pears and spooning with syrup once. Chill pears in syrup.

In small mixing bowl, mix ricotta, sugar and vanilla. Stir in dried fruit and cherries. Cover and chill for at least 3 hours. Remove pears from syrup with slotted spoon. Discard syrup. Place each pear half on lettuce-lined plate. Fill pear halves evenly with ricotta mixture to serve.

Twice-baked Yams

2 yams or sweet potatoes
  (8 to 10 oz. each)
⅓ cup chopped pecans
2 tablespoons butter or
  margarine
½ cup marshmallow cream
1 teaspoon grated orange peel
½ teaspoon salt

4 servings

Wash yams and pierce with fork. Place directly in oven on paper towel. Microwave at High for 8 to 10 minutes, or just until yams feel soft. Let cool slightly.

Cut baked yams in half length-wise and scoop out pulp, leaving about ¼-inch shells. Set shells and pulp aside.

In medium mixing bowl, combine pecans and butter. Microwave at High for 45 seconds to 1 minute, or until butter melts. Add yam pulp and remaining ingredients. Beat at medium speed of electric mixer until mixture is smooth. Pipe or spoon mixture evenly into shells. Arrange stuffed yams on plate. Microwave at High for 2 to 4 minutes, or until yams are hot, rotating plate once.

Stuffed Orange Cups

3 large oranges (9 to 10 oz. each)
1 can (18 oz.) sweet potatoes
¼ teaspoon ground coriander
⅛ teaspoon ground nutmeg
1 tablespoon butter or margarine
2 tablespoons sour cream
1 tablespoon packed brown sugar
⅛ teaspoon salt
  Dash pepper
¼ cup raisins, divided

6 servings

How to Microwave Stuffed Orange Cups

Cut each orange in half crosswise, angling knife in sawtooth fashion to form decorative edge. Squeeze and reserve 2 tablespoons juice from one orange half. Spoon out pulp of each half, leaving shells. Set shells aside. In a medium mixing bowl, combine sweet potatoes and reserved 2 tablespoons orange juice.

Sprinkle with coriander and nutmeg. Add butter. Cover with plastic wrap. Microwave at High for 4 to 5 minutes, or until mixture is hot, stirring once. Add sour cream, brown sugar, salt and pepper. Beat at medium speed of electric mixer until mixture is smooth. Stir in 2 tablespoons raisins.

Spoon sweet potato mixture evenly into orange shells. Arrange stuffed oranges around outside of plate. Microwave at High for 3 to 5 minutes, or until hot, rotating plate once. Sprinkle with remaining 2 tablespoons raisins.

Salmon-Cucumber Canapés

2 cucumbers (8-inch)
3 tablespoons chopped celery
2 tablespoons chopped onion
1 can (6¾ oz.) skinless,
   boneless salmon, drained
2 tablespoons sour cream
1 teaspoon lemon juice
½ teaspoon grated lemon peel
   Dash pepper
   Paprika

      1 dozen canapés

Slice each cucumber crosswise into six equal pieces. With small spoon or melon baller, scoop out center of each piece, leaving ¼-inch shell. Flatten ends of rounded pieces by cutting thin slices from green ends. Place pieces hollowed-sides-down on paper towel to drain.

In small mixing bowl, combine celery and onion. Cover with plastic wrap. Microwave at High for 1 to 2 minutes, or until vegetables are tender. Add remaining ingredients, except paprika. Mix well. Fill cucumber cups evenly with salmon mixture. Arrange canapés on plate. Microwave at High for 3 to 6 minutes, or until canapés are warm, rotating plate once. Sprinkle with paprika to serve. (Canapés may also be refrigerated and served chilled.)

Smoked Salmon ▲
Potato Cups

- 1 lb. medium red potatoes (about 2-inch diameter)
- ¼ cup water
- ⅓ cup sour cream
- 2 tablespoons mayonnaise or salad dressing
- 1 tablespoon finely chopped onion
- 1½ teaspoons dried parsley flakes
- 1 teaspoon prepared horseradish
- 1 cup flaked smoked salmon

8 to 10 servings

In 2-quart casserole, combine potatoes and water. Cover. Microwave at High for 7 to 10 minutes, or just until potatoes are tender. Let stand, covered, for 1 minute. Rinse in cold water. Drain and set aside. In small mixing bowl, combine remaining ingredients, except salmon. Mix well. Stir in salmon. Cover and refrigerate.

Cut each potato in half. With small spoon or melon baller, scoop out centers, leaving ¼ to ½-inch shells. Reserve centers for future use, if desired. Fill potato cups evenly with salmon mixture. Chill for at least 1 hour. Top with paprika or snipped fresh parsley, if desired.

Wine-steamed Mussels in Shells ▲

Use 1 lb. fresh mussels or clams. Scrub outsides of shells thoroughly. Remove beards from mussels. Discard any broken or open shells. Soak in salted spring water for at least 3 hours to clean. Discard any open or floating shells. Rinse and drain.

In 2-quart casserole, place ½ cup white wine and ½ teaspoon bouquet garni seasoning. Microwave at High for 2 to 3½ minutes, or until mixture boils. Add mussels or clams. Cover. Microwave at High as directed in chart (below), or until shells open, stirring once.

Strain broth through several layers of cheesecloth. Add 2 tablespoons butter or margarine to broth, stirring until melted. Garnish broth with snipped fresh parsley. Serve mussels with broth or melted butter, if desired.

4 to 6 servings

Amount	Microwave at High
1 lb. mussels (about 20)	1½ to 3 minutes
1 lb. clams (about 12 to 15)	3 to 5½ minutes

Creamy Squash ▲ & Apple Soup

1 buttercup squash (about 2½ lbs.)
1 medium apple, cored, peeled and sliced
¼ cup finely chopped onion
3 tablespoons butter or margarine
¼ teaspoon ground nutmeg
¼ teaspoon curry powder (optional)
¼ teaspoon salt
1 tablespoon all-purpose flour
½ cup half-and-half
¼ cup ready-to-serve chicken broth

2 to 4 servings

How to Microwave Creamy Squash & Apple Soup

Cut top off of squash. Set top aside. Remove and discard seeds and fiber. Cover squash with plastic wrap. Microwave at High for 6 to 8 minutes, or until pulp is tender, rotating once. Let stand, covered.

Combine apple, onion and butter in medium mixing bowl. Microwave at High for 5 to 6½ minutes, or until onions and apple are soft, stirring once. Set aside.

Pork-stuffed Butternut Squash ▲

1 butternut squash (about 2¾ lbs.)
1 lb. pork tenderloin, trimmed and cut into ½-inch cubes
1 small zucchini (5 to 6 oz.) cut in half lengthwise, then into ½-inch slices
1 can (8 oz.) tomato sauce

2 tablespoons thinly sliced green onion
½ teaspoon salt
¼ teaspoon dried marjoram leaves
⅛ teaspoon dried thyme leaves
⅛ teaspoon pepper

4 servings

Cut squash in half lengthwise. Remove and discard seeds and fiber. Wrap each squash half in plastic wrap. Microwave at High for 8 to 14 minutes, or until pulp is tender, rearranging halves once. Set aside.

Combine remaining ingredients in 1½-quart casserole. Mix well. Cover. Microwave at High for 10 to 13 minutes, or until pork is tender and cooked through, stirring 2 or 3 times. Set aside. Scoop pulp from center of each squash half, leaving ½-inch shell. Chop pulp and stir into pork mixture. Microwave pork mixture at High for 1 to 2 minutes, or until hot. Spoon mixture evenly into squash shells.

Scoop out ½ to ⅔ cup of tender squash pulp with spoon, leaving shell at least ¼ inch thick. Set shell aside.

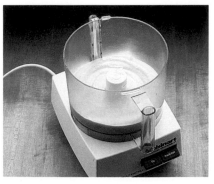

Place apple mixture, squash pulp, nutmeg, curry powder and salt in food processor or blender. Purée. Mix in flour. Blend in half-and-half and broth. Pour mixture into medium mixing bowl.

Microwave at High for 4 to 6½ minutes, or until mixture thickens and bubbles, stirring with whisk 2 or 3 times. Pour soup into squash shell. Use reserved top as lid for squash shell, if desired.

Italian Spaghetti Squash

1 spaghetti squash (4 to 4½ lbs.); or 2 small spaghetti squash (2 to 2¼ lbs. each)
½ lb. ground beef
¼ cup chopped green pepper
2 tablespoons finely chopped onion
1 jar (15½ oz.) spaghetti sauce
¼ teaspoon salt
¼ teaspoon dried basil leaves
   Dash pepper
   Grated Parmesan cheese (optional)

4 servings

With sharp knife, pierce squash rind deeply several times to allow steam to escape. Place squash on paper towel in oven. Microwave at High for 15 to 25 minutes, or until squash skin yields to pressure, turning squash after every 5 minutes. Set aside.

Crumble ground beef into a 1½-quart casserole. Add green pepper and onion. Cover. Microwave at High for 3 to 4½ minutes, or until meat is no longer pink, stirring once to break apart. Drain. Stir in spaghetti sauce, salt, basil and pepper. Cover with paper towel. Microwave at High for 5 to 8 minutes, or until mixture is hot and flavors are blended, stirring once. Set aside.

Cut squash in half lengthwise. Scoop out and discard seeds and fiber. Twist long strands of flesh with fork. Spoon sauce evenly into squash halves. Sprinkle with Parmesan cheese to serve.

66

Turkey & Vegetable-filled Eggplant

½ lb. ground turkey
1 medium eggplant (about 1½ lbs.)
1 can (16 oz.) whole tomatoes, cut up and drained
¼ cup chopped onion
1 tablespoon olive oil
¾ cup onion-garlic croutons
⅓ cup frozen peas
½ teaspoon Italian seasoning
½ teaspoon salt
⅛ teaspoon pepper
½ cup finely shredded mozzarella cheese

2 to 4 servings

Crumble turkey into 1-quart casserole. Cover. Microwave at High for 2½ to 4 minutes, or until turkey is firm, stirring once to break apart. Drain and set aside.

Cut eggplant in half lengthwise. With a thin, flexible knife, cut around edge of pulp. Scoop out pulp, leaving ¼-inch shells. Chop pulp coarsely and set aside. Place eggplant shells hollowed-sides-up in 9-inch square baking dish. Set aside.

In 1½-quart casserole, combine chopped pulp, tomatoes, onion and olive oil. Cover. Microwave at High for 9 to 12 minutes, or until eggplant is tender, stirring twice. Mix in turkey, croutons, peas, Italian seasoning, salt and pepper. Spoon mixture evenly into eggplant shells. Cover with wax paper. Microwave at High for 8 to 10 minutes, or until shells are tender, rotating dish once or twice. Sprinkle with mozzarella cheese and let stand for 1 to 2 minutes, or until cheese melts.

Curry Chicken & Pineapple

- 1 lb. boneless whole chicken breasts, skinned, cut into ¾-inch pieces
- ¼ cup white wine
- 1 teaspoon curry powder
- 1 pineapple (about 4 lbs.)
- 1½ cups hot cooked rice
- ⅓ cup sliced celery
- ⅓ cup shredded carrot
- 2 tablespoons sliced green onion

Dressing:
- ½ cup plain yogurt
- ¼ cup mayonnaise
- 2 tablespoons snipped fresh parsley
- 1 teaspoon sugar
- ¾ teaspoon salt

- ¼ cup cashews

4 to 6 servings

In 1-quart casserole, combine chicken pieces, wine and curry powder. Mix well. Cover. Microwave at High for 4 to 7 minutes, or until chicken is no longer pink, stirring once or twice. Drain mixture and place in medium mixing bowl. Set aside.

Cut pineapple in half lengthwise, leaving leafy portions attached. With thin, flexible knife, loosen and remove fruit, leaving ½-inch shells. Cut and discard core from fruit. Drain pineapple juice from shells. Set shells upright on 12-inch round platter. Set aside. Chop fruit and add to chicken mixture. Add rice, celery, carrot and onion. Set mixture aside.

Combine all dressing ingredients in small mixing bowl. Mix well. Pour over chicken mixture. Toss salad to coat with dressing. Spoon salad into pineapple shells. Microwave at High for 5 to 6 minutes, or until salad is warm, rotating platter once. Top with cashews.

TIP: An excellent salad for party buffets. Serve hot or chilled.

Cabbage Head Salad

⅓ cup sugar
¾ teaspoon salt
½ teaspoon dry mustard
2 tablespoons cider vinegar
¼ cup half-and-half
1 egg yolk

1 large cabbage (3½ lbs.)
1 cup shredded zucchini
½ cup shredded carrot
2 tablespoons finely chopped onion

6 to 8 servings

TIP: Cabbage Head Salad in its own container is a perfect dish to make ahead and bring to pot-luck buffets: no dish to wash or return.

How to Microwave Cabbage Head Salad

Combine sugar, salt and dry mustard in 2-cup measure. Add vinegar. Mix well. Blend in half-and-half and egg yolk. Microwave at 50% (Medium) for 4 to 5 minutes, or until mixture is very hot and slightly thickened, stirring twice. Chill for at least 1 hour.

Cut ¾-inch slice from leafy side of cabbage head. Reserve cut cabbage for salad. With sharp knife, hollow out inside of cabbage, leaving ¾-inch shell. Place reserved cut cabbage in a food processor or blender, and process until finely chopped.

Place chopped cabbage in medium mixing bowl. Add zucchini, carrot and onion. Add dressing. Toss well to mix. Spoon salad into cabbage shell. Serve immediately or chill until serving time. Refill with additional salad as needed.

Chinese Cabbage Rolls

2¼ to 2½ lbs. Chinese cabbage (celery-type)

Filling:

 1 lb. unseasoned ground pork
 ½ cup chopped fresh mushrooms
 ¼ cup chopped onion
 1 cup cooked rice
 ⅓ cup shredded carrot
 1 egg, slightly beaten
 2 tablespoons soy sauce
 ¼ teaspoon salt
 ¼ teaspoon ground ginger
 ¼ teaspoon five-spice powder (optional)
 ¼ teaspoon pepper
 ⅛ teaspoon garlic powder

Sauce:

 ½ cup water
 1 tablespoon soy sauce
 1½ teaspoons cornstarch
 ¾ teaspoon instant beef bouillon granules
 ¼ teaspoon sugar
    Dash pepper

4 servings

How to Microwave Chinese Cabbage Rolls

Cut stem end off cabbage to release leaves. Remove 8 large outer leaves and set aside. Slice enough inner leaves (crosswise, about ¼ inch thick) to equal 1 cup. Reserve remaining inner leaves for future use, if desired. Place sliced cabbage in 2-quart casserole.

Crumble pork over sliced cabbage. Add mushrooms and onion. Cover. Microwave at High for 6 to 9 minutes, or until pork is no longer pink, stirring twice to break apart. Drain. Place meat mixture in medium mixing bowl. Add remaining filling ingredients. Mix well and set aside.

Place one large cabbage leaf on each of four 15-inch lengths of plastic wrap. Spoon meat mixture evenly onto leaves. Top each with another leaf. Roll plastic wrap around leaves, leaving ends of wrap unsealed.

Arrange wrapped cabbage rolls on 12-inch round platter. Microwave at High for 8 to 11 minutes, or until stalk portion of each leaf is fork-tender, rearranging rolls once. Set aside.

Combine all sauce ingredients in 2-cup measure. Mix until smooth. Microwave at High for 2 to 3 minutes, or until mixture is thickened and translucent, stirring twice. Serve sauce over cabbage rolls.

Herbed Stuffed Onions

 4 large red or yellow onions (10 to 12 oz. each)
 ¼ cup chopped celery
 1 teaspoon dried parsley flakes
 ¼ teaspoon poultry seasoning
 3 tablespoons butter or margarine
1¼ cups herb-seasoned stuffing mix
 ¼ cup plus 3 tablespoons water, divided

4 servings

Cut ¾-inch slice from top of each onion. Cut small slice from root ends to allow onions to stand upright. Peel onions. With a thin, flexible knife, loosen center of each onion. Scoop out center portions, leaving ¼-inch shells. (Onion centers may be chopped and frozen for later use.) Place onion shells cut-sides-up in pie plate. Set aside.

In small mixing bowl, combine celery, parsley, poultry seasoning and butter. Cover with plastic wrap. Microwave at High for 2 to 3 minutes, or until celery is tender. Stir in stuffing mix. Sprinkle with 3 tablespoons water, stirring to moisten. Spoon stuffing mixture evenly into onion shells. Pour remaining ¼ cup water around onions in pie plate. Cover with plastic wrap. Microwave at High for 9 to 12 minutes, or until onions are tender, rotating and rearranging onions once. Let stuffed onions stand, covered, for 3 to 5 minutes before serving.

Stuffed Fennel Stalks

    1 fennel bulb
    3 tablespoons finely chopped
      onion
    3 tablespoons butter or
      margarine
1⅓ cups cornbread stuffing mix
    1 teaspoon dried parsley
      flakes
      Dash salt
    1 egg, beaten
    ½ cup tomato purée
    1 teaspoon dried basil leaves
    1 teaspoon olive oil

4 servings

Cut green upper stems and feathery leaves from fennel bulb. Cut thin slice from base of bulb to release stalks. Separate stalks. Remove coarse fibers on outside surface of largest stalks, as directed (right). Cut very large stalks lengthwise into 2 or 3 shells. Set aside.

In small mixing bowl, combine onion and butter. Microwave at High for 1½ to 2½ minutes, or until onion is tender. Stir in stuffing mix, parsley flakes and salt. Mix in egg. Spoon mixture evenly onto fennel shells, pressing lightly. Place shells in 10-inch square casserole. Add water. Set aside.

In 1-cup measure, mix tomato purée, basil and olive oil. Microwave at High for 1 to 2 minutes, or until hot. Spoon mixture over stuffing. Cover. Microwave at 70% (Medium High) for 7 to 10 minutes, or until fennel is tender, rotating casserole once.

How to Remove Coarse Fibers

Use a small knife to cut into, but not through, the top of largest fennel stalks.

Hold fibers against knife blade with finger and pull downward to remove coarse fibers.

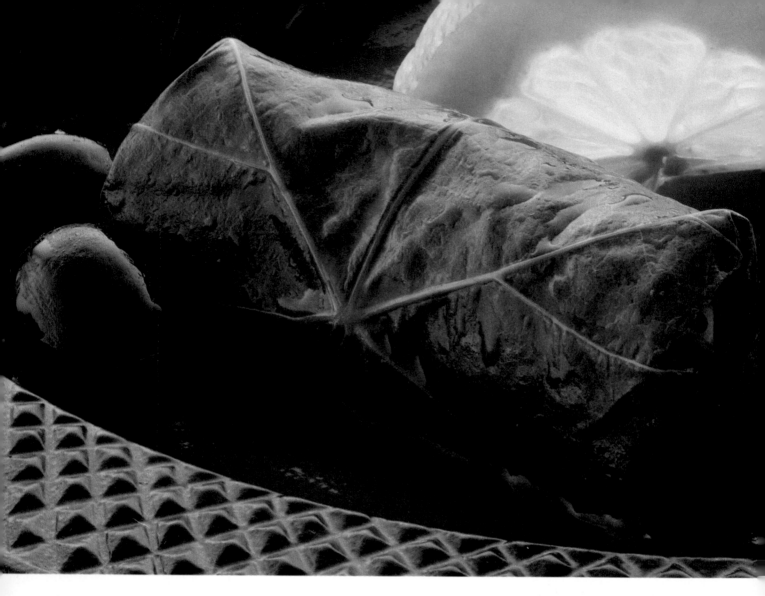

Grape Leaves with Lamb Filling

Filling:
- 1 lb. ground lamb
- ¼ cup finely chopped onion
- ¼ cup chopped green pepper
- 1 clove garlic, minced
- 1 cup cooked rice
- ¼ cup raisins
- 2 tablespoons snipped fresh parsley
- 2 tablespoons pine nuts
- 2 tablespoons catsup
- ½ teaspoon bouquet garni seasoning
- ½ teaspoon salt
- ¼ teaspoon ground allspice
- ⅛ teaspoon cayenne

- 1 jar (8 oz.) grape leaves, rinsed and drained
- 2 tablespoons water
- 1 small lemon, sliced

Sauce:
- 1 can (8 oz.) tomato sauce
- ½ teaspoon sugar
  Dash salt
  Dash ground cinnamon

6 servings

How to Microwave Grape Leaves with Lamb Filling

Crumble ground lamb into 2-quart casserole. Add onion, green pepper and garlic. Cover. Microwave at High for 4 to 7 minutes, or until lamb is no longer pink, stirring once to break apart. Drain. Add remaining filling ingredients. Mix well.

Lay one grape leaf flat with vein-side-up. Spoon about 1 table-spoon filling onto center of leaf. Fold in point of leaf, then sides. Roll up leaf, enclosing filling. Repeat with remaining filling to form 2½ to 3 dozen grape leaves. Reserve any extra grape leaves.

Place filled leaves in 10-inch square casserole. Sprinkle with water. Top filled leaves with lemon slices, then with damp reserved grape leaves. Microwave at High for 8 to 12 minutes, or until leaves are hot, rotating dish once. Set aside.

Combine all sauce ingredients in 2-cup measure. Microwave at High for 2 to 2½ minutes, or until mixture is hot and bubbly, stirring once. Spoon sauce onto plate and arrange filled grape leaves over sauce. Garnish with additional lemon slices, if desired.

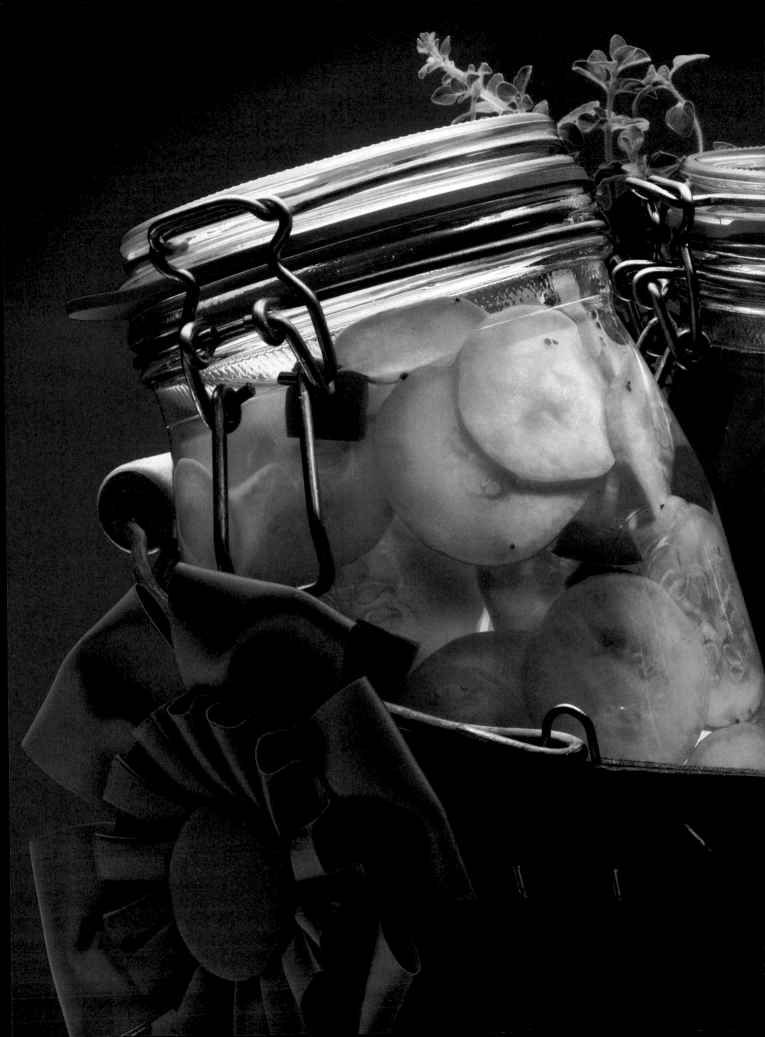

Blue Ribbon Extras

Yellow Summer Squash Pickles
Pickled Eggs
Christmas Overnight Pickles

Oregano

Sage

Mint

Cilantro

Basil

Fresh Herbs for Drying

Herb:	Use in:	Complements:
Basil	Egg dishes, salads, tomato & cream sauces, pesto, vegetable soups, vegetable dishes	Beef, lamb, pork, veal, poultry, fish
Chervil	Egg dishes, creamed mixtures & soups, vegetable dishes	Poultry, fish & seafood
Cilantro*	Mexican dishes & sauces, Chinese & Italian dishes	Beef, lamb, pork, veal, poultry, fish & seafood
Dill weed	Soups & stews, sauces & butters, pickles, vegetable dishes	Beef, lamb, pork, veal, poultry, fish & seafood
Marjoram	Meatballs, meatloaf, salads, soups, stuffings, egg dishes, vegetable dishes	Beef, lamb, pork, veal, poultry, fish & seafood
Mint	Desserts, beverages, fruit compotes, jellies	Lamb, veal, fish
Oregano	Chili, spaghetti sauce, tomato dishes, soups, stews, vegetable dishes, pizza	Beef, lamb, pork, veal, poultry, fish & seafood
Parsley	Stuffings, sauces, soups, stews, vegetable dishes	Beef, lamb, pork, veal, poultry, fish & seafood
Rosemary	Egg dishes, vegetable dishes, stuffings, soups, stews	Beef, lamb, pork, veal, poultry, fish
Sage	Sausages, soups, stuffings, egg dishes, vegetable dishes	Pork, veal, poultry, fish
Tarragon	Egg dishes, meat sauces, poultry or fish sauces, salads, salad dressings, soups, stews	Beef, veal, poultry, fish & seafood
Thyme	Chowders, soufflés, omelets, vegetable dishes, stuffings, soups, stews	Beef, lamb, pork, poultry, fish & seafood

*also: Chinese or Italian parsley, fresh coriander

Fresh-dried Herbs

Whether you grow your own fresh herbs or buy them at the supermarket, you probably have more than you can use. Save your surplus herbs by drying them quickly in the microwave oven. Herbs dried in the microwave retain their fresh, bright color, fragrance and characteristic leaf shapes.

Make your own flavor combinations by mixing equal parts of fresh-dried herbs. For poultry, seafood or salad dressings, try tarragon, chervil and parsley. Complement meat with a mixture of thyme, sage and marjoram.

Drying Fresh Herbs in the Microwave

Wash and thoroughly dry one bunch of fresh herbs selected from chart (page 79). Strip leaves from stems. Discard stems and tear larger leaves in ½ to ¾-inch pieces. Loosely pack enough herbs to equal ½ cup. Place one paper towel on plate. Sprinkle herbs evenly over towel.

Place ½ cup cold water in 1-cup measure. Place water next to plate in microwave oven. Microwave at High for 3¼ to 4 minutes, or just until leaves begin to feel dry and papery, tossing with fingers after first minute, and then after every 45 seconds. Watch closely to avoid over-drying.

Remove herbs and sprinkle evenly onto another paper towel. (Repeat procedure for additional herbs, if desired.) Let air-dry for 24 hours to complete drying. Store in airtight container in cool, dark place when completely dry. Slightly crush dried herbs before measuring for use in recipes.

Italian Herbs

1 tablespoon dried parsley
  leaves (opposite)
1 tablespoon dried oregano
  leaves (opposite)
1 tablespoon dried basil leaves
  (opposite)
1 teaspoon dried thyme leaves,
  (opposite)
2 teaspoons dried marjoram
  leaves (opposite)
¼ teaspoon dried crushed red
  pepper

About ¼ cup

Combine all ingredients in small
bowl. Mix well. Store in covered
container in cool dark place.
Slightly crush mixture before
using. Use herbs on meats and
poultry, and for seasoning Italian
sauces and pizza.

Herb-seasoned Salt

2 tablespoons salt
1 tablespoon dried parsley
  flakes (opposite)
1 tablespoon dried basil leaves
  (opposite)
1 teaspoon dried dill weed
  (opposite)
½ teaspoon onion powder
¼ teaspoon garlic powder

About ¼ cup

Combine all ingredients in a small
bowl. Crush mixture in mortar with
pestle, or place mixture in blender
and process until very fine. Serve
as all-purpose seasoning.

Poultry Herb Medley

2 tablespoons dried rosemary
  leaves (opposite)
1 tablespoon dried marjoram
  leaves (opposite)
1 tablespoon dried thyme leaves
  (opposite)

¼ cup

Combine all ingredients in small
bowl. Mix well. Store in covered
container in cool dark place.
Slightly crush mixture before
using. Use medley on poultry,
lamb or pork.

TIP: Dry ½ cup celery leaves in the same way as fresh herbs (opposite).
Use dried celery leaves in soups, stews, main dishes and sauces.

81

Softening Butter

Butter and margarine melt and soften quickly because they have a high fat content, which attracts microwave energy. To soften butter without melting it: place butter in small bowl or on plate, and microwave at 30% (Medium Low) as directed in chart (below), checking after every 15 seconds.

Amount	Microwave at 30% (Medium Low)
2 tablespoons	15 to 30 seconds
¼ cup	15 to 45 seconds
½ cup	15 seconds to 1 minute

TIPS: Pack butter into crocks or butter molds for serving. Or use a pastry tube to pipe butter onto wax paper into individual butter pats. Chill until firm.

Use softened butter for spreads, for sweet and savory breads, or as a topping for hot cooked vegetables. For fluffy whipped butter, beat using an electric mixer.

How to Microwave Flavored Butters

Microwave ½ cup butter or margarine in small mixing bowl as directed in chart (above), or until softened.

Blend in additional ingredients for desired flavor (opposite).

Serve flavored butters as directed (opposite); store in refrigerator no longer than 2 weeks.

Flavored Butters

Flavor & yield	To ½ cup butter, blend in:	Serving suggestions
Almond-Peach Butter about ¾ cup	¼ cup ground almonds, 2 table-spoons peach preserves, 1 table-spoon Amaretto	Toast, Danish pastries, quick breads
Deviled Butter about ½ cup	1 teaspoon dry mustard, ¼ tea-spoon cayenne, ¼ teaspoon paprika, ⅛ teaspoon garlic powder	Meats, poultry, fish or seafood, hot cooked pasta, vegetables, cornbread
Fruit Preserve Butter about ⅔ cup	⅓ cup powdered sugar, 1 tablespoon of desired fruit preserves (straw-berry, blackberry, pineapple, etc.)	Toast, pancakes, waffles, French toast, croissants, quick breads
Honey-Pecan Butter about ¾ cup	¼ cup honey, 2 tablespoons chopped pecans, ⅛ teaspoon ground nutmeg	Toast, pancakes, waffles, French toast, quick breads
Lemon-Chive Butter about ½ cup	2 teaspoons freeze-dried chives, ½ teaspoon grated lemon peel, 6 drops hot red pepper sauce	Fish or seafood, hot cooked vegetables
Orange-Cinnamon Butter about ¾ cup	2 tablespoons packed brown sugar, 1 tablespoon orange juice, 1 tea-spoon grated orange peel, ¼ tea-spoon ground cinnamon	Toast, pancakes, waffles, French toast, quick breads
Parsley-Herb Butter about ½ cup	1 tablespoon fresh snipped parsley, 2 teaspoons finely chopped shallot, ¼ teaspoon dried marjoram leaves, ⅛ teaspoon dried thyme leaves	Steaks, dinner breads, hot cooked pasta, vegetables
Blue Cheese-Walnut Butter about ¾ cup	2 oz. crumbled blue cheese, 2 tablespoons chopped walnuts, ¼ teaspoon Worcestershire sauce, dash pepper	Steaks, savory crackers

Softening Cream Cheese

In small mixing bowl, microwave cream cheese as directed in chart (below), or until softened. DO NOT microwave cream cheese in the foil wrapper. For use in dips and spreads, blend softened cream cheese with favorite flavors, as directed in chart (opposite).

TIP: Cream cheese softens quickly in the microwave and spreads easily. Softened cheese is easier to blend in your favorite appetizer, main dish or dessert recipe.

Amount	Power setting	Microwave Time
1 pkg. (3 oz.)	High	15 to 30 seconds
1 pkg. (8 oz.)	50% (Medium)	1½ to 3 minutes

How to Microwave Flavored Cream Cheeses

Microwave 8 oz. cream cheese in small mixing bowl as directed in chart (above), stirring once or twice.

Blend in additional ingredients for desired flavor (opposite).

Serve flavored cream cheeses as directed (opposite); store cream cheese as recommended.

Flavored Cream Cheeses

Flavor & yield	To 8 oz. cream cheese blend in:	Serving suggestions	Store up to:
Cheddar & Chive Cream Cheese about 1¼ cups	½ cup finely shredded Cheddar cheese, 1 tablespoon sliced green onion, 1 teaspoon freeze-dried chives, ⅛ teaspoon garlic powder	Dip for vegetables; topping for hot cooked vegetables; spread for crackers, bread	2 weeks
Cocoa Cream Cheese Frosting about 1¼ cups	½ cup powdered sugar, 2 tablespoons cocoa, ½ teaspoon vanilla	Frosting for graham crackers, brownies, bars, cakes	2 weeks
Italian Herb Cream Cheese about 1 cup	2 tablespoons fresh snipped parsley, ½ teaspoon Italian seasoning	Spread for sandwiches or crackers; topping for hot cooked vegetables	2 weeks
Lemon-Basil Cream Cheese about 1¼ cups	2 teaspoons lemon juice, ½ teaspoon dried basil leaves (crushed), ¼ teaspoon garlic powder	Dip for vegetables; spread for bagels, French bread, cheese croissants	2 weeks
Mustard Relish Cream Cheese about 1¼ cups	2 tablespoons sweet relish, 1 tablespoon chopped onion, 2 teaspoons Dijon mustard	Spread for bagels, sandwiches, crackers	2 weeks
Orange Spice Cream Cheese about 1 cup	2 tablespoons sugar, 2 tablespoons orange juice, 1 teaspoon grated orange peel, ⅛ teaspoon ground allspice	Spread for fruit muffins, bagels, croissants, quick breads	2 weeks
Red Wine Onion Cream Cheese about 1¼ cups	2 tablespoons chopped onion, 2 tablespoons red wine, ⅛ teaspoon salt, dash pepper	Dip for vegetables; spread for crackers	2 weeks
Strawberry Cream Cheese about 1⅓ cups	½ cup fresh sliced strawberries, 2 tablespoons sugar, 1 teaspoon vanilla	Dip for fruit; spread for pound cakes, quick breads	3 days

Chocolate Pinwheel Spread

½ cup butter or margarine,
    softened (page 82)
1 pkg. (3 oz.) cream cheese,
    softened (page 84)
1 cup powdered sugar
¼ cup chocolate fudge topping
    Chocolate shot (optional)

One 6-inch roll

TIP: Serve spread with crois-
sants, pastries or quick breads.
Store remaining spread in refrigerator for no longer than
2 weeks.

How to Microwave Chocolate Pinwheel Spread

Blend butter and cream cheese in small mixing bowl. Reserve ¼ cup of mixture in another small bowl. Add powdered sugar to larger portion of butter mixture. Mix until smooth and creamy. Line baking sheet with wax paper.

Spread sugar mixture on baking sheet, forming 6 × 9-inch rec-tangle, about ¼ inch thick. Chill for 15 minutes. Blend topping into reserved ¼ cup butter mixture.

Spread fudge mixture evenly over chilled sugar layer. Chill for 1 hour to firm. Starting on short side, lift paper and roll until layer begins to roll tightly, enclosing fudge layer.

Lift and peel back paper while rolling, until roll is complete. Sprinkle with chocolate shot. Chill for at least 2 hours before slicing.

Mocha Variation: Follow recipe opposite, except blend 1 teaspoon instant coffee crystals with 1 teaspoon hot water and add to fudge-butter mixture.

Pickles, Relishes & Condiments

Putting up pickles and relishes once meant hours of effort at harvest time. With most ingredients available year 'round, modern cooks microwave small batches as they are needed. Experiment with a variety of pickles, your own homemade salsa, or trend-setting specialty mustards which add spice to meals and cost less than those purchased from gourmet food shops.

The recipes on pages 88-97 are packed into sterilized jars after microwaving. They are not pressure- or water bath-canned, so they do require refrigeration.

Mixed Pickle Relish

1 cup peeled, seeded and chopped cucumber	2 teaspoons dry mustard
1 cup chopped onion	½ teaspoon grated fresh gingerroot
1 cup chopped red pepper	¼ teaspoon ground turmeric
1 cup chopped green pepper	⅛ teaspoon ground allspice
1 tablespoon pickling salt	⅛ teaspoon cayenne
⅔ cup sugar	1 clove garlic, minced
½ cup white wine vinegar	

1-pint jar

In colander, place cucumber, onion, red and green peppers. Sprinkle with salt. Toss lightly to mix. Let colander stand over bowl for 1½ hours, stirring occasionally.

Place salted vegetables in 1½-quart casserole. Add remaining ingredients. Mix well. Microwave at High for 20 to 30 minutes, or until mixture thickens slightly, stirring twice. Spoon mixture into sterilized 1-pint jar. Cover and refrigerate overnight before serving. Store relish in refrigerator for no longer than 1 month.

Christmas Overnight Pickles

1 large cucumber (¾ lb.)
  peeled and cut crosswise
  into 3 pieces
4 whole allspice
4 whole cloves
½ cup water
½ cup cider vinegar
½ cup sugar
¼ teaspoon salt
¼ teaspoon ground nutmeg
½ teaspoon red food coloring
½ teaspoon green food coloring

4 to 6 servings

How to Microwave Christmas Overnight Pickles

Scoop out and discard seeds from cucumber, slice hollow pieces into ¼-inch rings. Divide cucumber rings evenly between two plastic food-storage bags. Add 2 allspice and 2 cloves to each bag. Set aside.

Combine remaining ingredients, except food colorings, in 2-cup measure. Microwave at High for 2 to 5 minutes, or until mixture boils, stirring once to dissolve sugar and salt. Divide mixture into two portions. Stir red coloring into one portion. Stir green coloring into remaining portion. Cool slightly.

Pour red vinegar mixture over cucumbers in one food-storage bag. Pour green vinegar mixture into remaining bag. Tie securely and refrigerate bags overnight. Drain pickles before serving. Store in refrigerator for no longer than 3 days.

Yellow Summer Squash Pickles

3 cups thinly sliced yellow summer squash
½ cup coarsely chopped red pepper
1 small onion, thinly sliced and separated into rings
8 whole peppercorns
1 large clove garlic, cut into quarters (optional)
1 cup white wine vinegar
⅔ cup sugar
2 teaspoons pickling salt
¼ teaspoon celery seed
¼ teaspoon mustard seed

Two 1-pint jars

In medium mixing bowl, mix squash, red pepper and onion. Divide mixture and pack evenly into two sterilized 1-pint jars. Place 4 peppercorns and 2 garlic quarters in each jar. Set aside.

Combine remaining ingredients in 2-cup measure. Microwave at High for 2 to 5 minutes, or until mixture boils, stirring once to dissolve sugar and salt. Pour mixture evenly into jars. Cover and refrigerate for at least 5 days before serving. Store in refrigerator for no longer than 1 month.

Pickled Eggs ▶

Juice from 1 can (16 oz.)
    sliced beets
Water
⅔ cup cider vinegar
3 tablespoons packed brown
    sugar
¾ teaspoon salt
6 whole cloves
6 whole allspice
6 whole peppercorns
1 medium onion, thinly sliced
6 hard-cooked eggs, peeled

6 servings

Add enough water to beet juice to measure 1 cup. (Reserve beets for future use, if desired.) In medium mixing bowl, combine beet juice mixture, vinegar, sugar, salt, cloves, allspice and peppercorns. Add onion. Cover with plastic wrap. Microwave at High for 6 to 8 minutes, or until onion is tender-crisp, stirring once. Add eggs. Cover and refrigerate for 1 to 2 days, turning occasionally to assure even-colored eggs. Drain and slice eggs. Serve on platter or in salads.

Pickled Green Beans

1 pkg. (10 oz.) frozen cut, or
    French-cut, green beans
1 small onion, cut in half
    lengthwise and thinly sliced
½ cup sliced black olives
1 cup white vinegar
⅔ cup sugar
2 teaspoons pickling salt
¼ teaspoon dried tarragon
    leaves or dried dill weed

Three ½-pint jars

In medium mixing bowl, microwave beans at High for 4 to 6 minutes, or until defrosted, breaking apart once. Drain thoroughly. Add onion and black olives. Mix well. Divide mixture and pack evenly into three sterilized ½-pint jars. Set aside.

Combine remaining ingredients in 2-cup measure. Microwave at High for 2 to 5 minutes, or until mixture boils, stirring once to dissolve sugar and salt. Pour mixture evenly into jars. Cover and refrigerate for at least 5 days before serving. Store in refrigerator for no longer than 1 month.

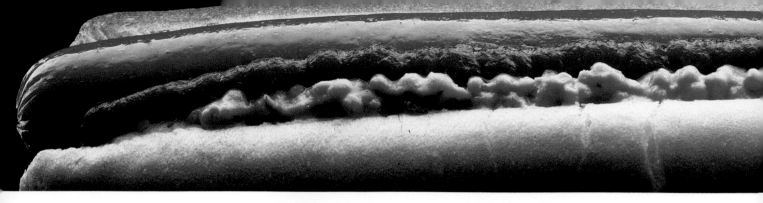

How to Microwave Basil-Onion Mustard

Basil-Onion Mustard

⅓ cup dry mustard
 3 tablespoons mustard seed,
   slightly crushed
 2 teaspoons dried basil leaves,
   divided
½ cup hot water
⅓ cup white wine vinegar
⅓ cup finely chopped onion
 1 tablespoon sugar
 2 teaspoons mixed pickling
   spices
 1 teaspoon salt

      ¾ to 1 cup mustard

Combine dry mustard, mustard seed and ½ teaspoon basil leaves in small mixing bowl. Add water. Mix well. Cover and set aside for 1 hour. Combine remaining 1½ teaspoons dried basil leaves and remaining ingredients in 1-quart casserole. Mix well. Cover. Microwave at High for 3 to 4 minutes, or until onion is tender. Let stand, covered, until cool.

Strain vinegar mixture into mustard mixture using wire strainer, pressing with back of spoon. Discard onion solids. Stir mustard mixture. Microwave, uncovered, at High for 4 to 5 minutes, or until mixture thickens slightly, stirring once.

Spoon mustard into sterilized jar. Cover and refrigerate overnight before serving. Store in refrigerator for no longer than 3 months. If desired, mix vinegar or water into cooled mustard to thin.

Tarrragon-Garlic Mustard: Follow recipe above, except substitute tarragon leaves for the basil, and 2 cloves garlic, (each cut into quarters), for the onion. Microwave as directed, or until garlic is tender.

Home-style ▲ Brown Mustard

⅓ cup dry mustard
3 tablespoons mustard seed, slightly crushed
½ cup hot water
¼ cup plus 2 tablespoons cider vinegar
⅓ cup coarsely chopped onion
3 tablespoons packed dark brown sugar
1 clove garlic, cut into quarters
1 teaspoon salt
½ teaspoon dill seed
¼ teaspoon dried marjoram leaves
⅛ teaspoon ground allspice
⅛ teaspoon ground cinnamon
6 whole peppercorns

1 cup mustard

In small mixing bowl, combine dry mustard and mustard seed. Add water and mix well. Cover and set aside for 1 hour. In 1-quart casserole, combine all remaining ingredients. Cover. Microwave at High for 3 to 4 minutes, or until onion is tender. Let mixture stand, covered, until cool.

Using wire strainer, strain vinegar mixture into dry mustard mixture, pressing with back of spoon. Discard onion solids. Stir mustard mixture. Microwave, uncovered, at High for 4 to 5 minutes, or until mixture thickens slightly, stirring once. Spoon into sterilized jar. Cover and refrigerate overnight before serving. Store in refrigerator for no longer than 3 months. If desired, mix vinegar or water into cooled mustard to thin.

Homemade Catsup ▲

2 medium fresh tomatoes (about 1 lb.), seeded and chopped
¼ cup chopped onion
1 clove garlic, minced
2 teaspoons vegetable oil
1 can (12 oz.) tomato paste
⅓ cup red wine vinegar
¼ cup light corn syrup
1½ teaspoons paprika
¾ teaspoon salt
¼ teaspoon cayenne
¼ teaspoon Worcestershire sauce
⅛ teaspoon ground cloves

2½ cups catsup

In 2-quart casserole, combine tomatoes, onion, garlic and vegetable oil. Microwave at High for 7 to 9 minutes, or until onion is very tender, stirring once. Place mixture in food processor or blender and purée. Mix in remaining ingredients. Return to casserole. Cover with wax paper. Microwave at High for 15 to 25 minutes, or until mixture reaches desired thickness, stirring 3 times. Spoon catsup into sterilized jar and refrigerate overnight before serving. Store catsup in refrigerator for no longer than 1 month.

Salsa

1½ cups chopped onion
1 cup chopped green pepper
1 to 2 cloves garlic, minced
1 tablespoon vegetable oil
1 can (28 oz.) whole tomatoes
1 can (15 oz.) tomato purée
1 can (4 oz.) chopped green chilies, drained
2 teaspoons fresh snipped cilantro, or 1 teaspoon dried cilantro leaves
1 teaspoon salt
1 teaspoon packed brown sugar
1 teaspoon chili powder
1 teaspoon ground cumin
¼ teaspoon dried crushed red pepper

Three 1-pint jars

In 3-quart casserole, combine onion, green pepper, garlic and oil. Cover. Microwave at High for 3 to 4 minutes, or until vegetables are tender-crisp, stirring once. Stir in remaining ingredients. Microwave, uncovered, at High for 15 to 20 minutes, or until mixture is hot and flavors are blended, stirring twice. Spoon mixture evenly into three sterilized 1-pint jars. Cover and refrigerate overnight before serving. Store salsa in refrigerator for no longer than 2 weeks.

Hot Salsa: Follow recipe above, except substitute 1 can (3.5 oz.) jalapeños, drained and chopped, for green chilies.

Blueberry-Kiwi
Refrigerator Jam ▲

2 cups peeled, cored and sliced
   kiwi fruit
2 cups frozen blueberries
2 cups sugar
1 pkg. (3 oz.) lemon gelatin

Three ½-pint jars

In medium mixing bowl, combine
kiwi fruit, blueberries and sugar.
Mix well. Microwave at High for 15
to 25 minutes, or until fruit is very
soft, stirring 3 or 4 times. Add
gelatin, stirring until dissolved.
Divide mixture evenly between
three sterilized ½-pint jars. Cover
and chill until set, about 2 hours.
Store jam in refrigerator for no
longer than 1 month.

Blueberry-Kiwi Light Jam: Follow recipe above, except substitute 1 pkg. (0.3 oz.) low-calorie
lemon gelatin for the 3-oz. pkg.

Cherry-Almond
Refrigerator Jam

4 cups frozen pitted dark sweet
   cherries
2 cups sugar
1 pkg. (3 oz.) cherry gelatin
¼ teaspoon almond extract

Three ½-pint jars

In medium mixing bowl, combine
cherries and sugar. Mix well.
Microwave at High for 15 to 25
minutes, or until cherries are very
soft, stirring 3 or 4 times. Add
gelatin, stirring until dissolved. Stir
in almond extract. Divide mixture
evenly between three sterilized
½-pint jars. Cover. Chill until set,
about 2 hours. Store jam in refrigerator for no longer than 1 month.

Cherry-Almond Light Jam: Follow recipe above, except substitute 1 pkg. (0.3 oz.) low-calorie
cherry gelatin for the 3-oz. pkg.

Strawberry-Rhubarb
Refrigerator Jam ▶

4 cups frozen cut-up rhubarb
2 cups sugar
1 pkg. (3 oz.) strawberry gelatin
2 teaspoons lemon juice

Three ½-pint jars

In medium mixing bowl, combine
rhubarb and sugar. Mix well.
Microwave at High for 15 to 25
minutes, or until rhubarb is very
soft, stirring 3 or 4 times. Add
gelatin, stirring until dissolved.
Mix in lemon juice. Divide mixture
evenly between three sterilized
½-pint jars. Cover. Chill until set,
about 2 hours. Store jam in refrigerator for no longer than 1 month.

**Strawberry-Rhubarb Light
Jam:** Follow recipe above, except substitute 1 pkg. (0.3 oz.)
low-calorie strawberry gelatin
for the 3-oz. pkg.

Pear Honey

　2　lbs. pears (4 medium),
　　　peeled and cored
2¼　cups sugar
　1　can (8 oz.) crushed
　　　pineapple
　1　tablespoon lemon juice
　½　teaspoon grated lemon peel

Three ½-pint jars

Cut each pear into 6 pieces. Place in food processor or blender. Process until finely chopped. Place chopped pears in 3-quart casserole. Stir in remaining ingredients. Mix well. Microwave at High for 30 to 40 minutes, or until pears are translucent and very tender, stirring 2 or 3 times. Divide mixture evenly between three sterilized ½-pint jars. Cover and refrigerate overnight before serving. Store in refrigerator for no longer than 1 month.

Apple Butter ▲

　3　lbs. cooking apples, peeled,
　　　cored and cut into quarters
　¼　cup apple cider
1½　cups granulated sugar
　½　cup packed brown sugar
　2　tablespoons cider vinegar
1½　to 1¾ teaspoons ground
　　　cinnamon
　¼　teaspoon ground allspice
　⅛　teaspoon ground nutmeg

Three ½-pint jars

Place apples in 3-quart casserole. Add apple cider. Cover. Microwave at High for 18 to 23 minutes, or until apples are very soft, stirring once or twice. Place mixture in food processor or blender, and process until smooth.

Return apple mixture to 3-quart casserole. Stir in remaining ingredients. Microwave, uncovered, at High for 30 to 45 minutes, or until mixture is very thick, stirring 3 or 4 times. Spoon mixture evenly into three sterilized ½-pint jars. Cover and refrigerate overnight before serving. Store Apple Butter in refrigerator for no longer than 1 month.

Brandied Fruit

¾ cup water
½ cup packed brown sugar
⅓ cup granulated sugar
½ teaspoon ground cinnamon
⅛ teaspoon ground allspice
⅛ teaspoon ground nutmeg
½ to ¾ cup brandy
1 cup dried apricots
1 cup dried apples
1 cup pitted prunes
½ cup raisins
¾ cup drained maraschino
   cherries (optional)

1 quart fruit

In medium mixing bowl, combine water, sugars, cinnamon, allspice and nutmeg. Mix well. Microwave at High for 4 to 6 minutes, or until mixture boils and sugar dissolves, stirring once.

Stir in remaining ingredients. Microwave at High for 9 to 14 minutes, or until apricots and apples are tender, stirring once or twice. Cover and refrigerate for at least 3 days before serving. Store in refrigerator for no longer than 3 weeks. Serve fruit over plain cake or ice cream, if desired.

Baked Brie Platter

Platter Presentations

Pretty and practical, these presentations give you flair without fuss. Assemble and microwave attractive appetizers, main dishes and desserts directly on the serving platter. No hasty last-minute garnishing. Most of the eye-pleasing arrangements can be made at your leisure, before the final microwaving.

TIP: Spread cooked rice or pasta on a platter. Top evenly with favorite cooked meat or vegetable sauce. Microwave at High until mixture is heated through. Top with cheese or garnish as desired.

Baked Brie Platter

1 tablespoon butter or
   margarine
2 tablespoons sliced almonds
1 wheel (8 oz.) Brie cheese
   (4½ × 1¼ inches)
   Apple wedges
   Red and green grapes
   Crackers
   Bread sticks

4 to 6 servings

In center of 12-inch platter, microwave butter at High for 45 seconds to 1 minute, or until melted. Add almonds, stirring to coat. Microwave at High for 6 to 8 minutes, or just until almonds begin to brown, stirring 2 or 3 times.

Move almonds to edge of platter. Place Brie in center. Spoon almonds onto top of Brie. Microwave at 50% (Medium) for 2 to 3½ minutes, or until Brie feels soft. To serve, arrange fruits, crackers and bread sticks on platter around Brie.

TIP: Frost grapes by brushing with egg white and sprinkling with granulated sugar. Let dry before arranging on platter.

Fresh Vegetable Platter & Dip ▲

2 cups fresh cauliflowerets
   (about 1½ lbs.)
2 cups fresh broccoli flowerets
   (about 1 lb.)
8 oz. fresh Brussels sprouts,
   trimmed

8 oz. fresh baby carrots
2 tablespoons water
1 recipe Cheese Dip in Pepper
   (page 56)

4 to 6 servings

Arrange vegetables in single layer on 12-inch round platter. Drizzle with water. Cover platter with vented plastic wrap. Microwave vegetables at High for 6 to 8 minutes, or until colors brighten, rotating platter once or twice. Drain through vent in plastic wrap. Refrigerate for at least 4 hours. Serve vegetables with Cheese Dip in Pepper.

Cheesy Seafood Snack Dip

2 pkgs. (8 oz. each) cream cheese, cut into 1-inch cubes
¾ cup cocktail sauce
1 can (6 oz.) crab meat, rinsed, drained and cartilage removed
1 can (4¼ oz.) medium shrimp, rinsed and drained
2 tablespoons sliced green onion

6 to 8 servings

Arrange cream cheese cubes in single layer on 12-inch round platter. Microwave at 50% (Medium) for 1½ to 3 minutes, or until cheese softens, rotating platter once or twice. Spread cream cheese into even layer on platter, to within 1 inch of edges. Top evenly with cocktail sauce. Sprinkle with remaining ingredients. Serve dip with assorted crackers.

Mexican Snack Dip

2 pkgs. (8 oz. each) cream cheese, cut into 1-inch cubes
1 cup refried beans
¾ cup taco sauce
1 cup shredded Cheddar cheese
½ cup seeded chopped tomato
¼ cup sliced black olives
2 tablespoons sliced green onion

6 to 8 servings

Arrange cream cheese cubes in single layer on 12-inch platter. Microwave at 50% (Medium) for 1½ to 3 minutes, or until cheese softens, rotating platter once or twice.

Spread cream cheese into even layer on platter, to within 1 inch of edges. Spread refried beans in even layer over cream cheese, to within ½ inch of edges. Top with taco sauce. Sprinkle with remaining ingredients. Serve snack platter with corn or tortilla chips.

Steamed Oriental Vegetables ▲

1 tablespoon sesame seed
4 cups fresh bean sprouts
1 jar (7 oz.) whole baby corn, drained
1 medium green pepper, cut into ¼-inch strips

1 cup sliced fresh mushrooms
2 tablespoons sherry
1 tablespoon soy sauce
¼ teaspoon ground ginger
⅛ teaspoon garlic salt
Dash pepper

4 to 6 servings

In small skillet, toast sesame seed conventionally over medium heat. Set aside. Spread sprouts in even layer on 12-inch round platter. Top with corn, green pepper and mushrooms. Set aside.

In 1-cup measure, mix sherry, soy sauce, ginger, garlic salt and pepper. Pour mixture evenly over vegetables. Cover with vented plastic wrap. Microwave at High for 6 to 9 minutes, or until pepper is tender-crisp, rotating platter once. Drain through vent in plastic wrap, if desired. Sprinkle toasted sesame seed over vegetables to serve.

Cheese Crisp Platter

1 tablespoon vegetable oil
1 flour tortilla (10-inch)
1 cup shredded Cheddar cheese
½ cup shredded Monterey Jack cheese
Sliced jalapeño peppers

4 servings

Heat oil conventionally in 12-inch skillet over medium-high heat. Add tortilla and fry until crisp and brown, turning over once. Remove from heat. Place tortilla on round platter. Sprinkle with cheeses and peppers. Microwave at 50% (Medium) for 3 to 5 minutes, or until cheeses melt, rotating platter once or twice.

Fruit & Sausage Brunch

¼ cup orange marmalade
2 tablespoons butter or
   margarine
¼ teaspoon lemon juice
8 wooden skewers (6-inch)
1 small pear, cored and cut into
   8 chunks
1 can (16 oz.) apricot halves in
   heavy syrup
8 maraschino cherries
1 large banana, cut crosswise
   into 8 pieces
8 medium strawberries
1 can (8 oz.) pineapple chunks
4 fully cooked Polish sausages,
   cut into halves and scored

4 servings

How to Microwave Fruit & Sausage Brunch

Combine marmalade, butter and lemon juice in small bowl. Microwave at High for 45 seconds to 1¼ minutes, or until butter melts, stirring twice. Set aside.

Thread ingredients on wooden skewer in following order: pear, apricot, cherry, another apricot, banana, strawberry and pineapple. Repeat to form 8 kabobs. Brush banana and pear chunks with marmalade mixture.

Place kabobs on 12-inch round platter, with pineapple chunks toward center and pears toward outside. Arrange sausage halves in pairs, alternating between pairs of kabobs. Cover with wax paper.

Microwave at High for 7 to 11 minutes, or until sausages are hot, rotating platter once or twice. Brush fruit with marmalade mixture before serving.

Save any extra apricot and pineapple chunks for future use. Apricots packed in heavy syrup are firmer and easier to thread onto skewers.

Ham & Turkey Platter ▲

1 round sheet lefse (about
   12-inch)
   Mustard (optional)
¼ lb. shaved fully cooked ham
¼ lb. shaved fully cooked turkey
½ cup finely shredded Cheddar
   cheese
1 tablespoon sliced green onion
   Tomato slices

2 to 4 servings

Place lefse on 12-inch platter.
Spread lightly with mustard. Arrange ham and turkey on one half
of lefse. Top meats with Cheddar
cheese and green onion. Fold
lefse over to enclose filling. Place
in center of platter. Microwave at
High for 2 to 5 minutes, or until
center feels very hot, rotating platter twice. Sprinkle lightly with additional Cheddar cheese and green
onion, if desired. Garnish with
tomato slices.

Sausage-stuffed Zucchini Platter

4 medium zucchini or yellow
   summer squash (6 to
   8 oz. each)
¾ lb. bulk Italian sausage
1 small onion, chopped

⅔ cup herb-seasoned
   stuffing mix
2 cups hot cooked rice
¼ to ½ cup salsa or taco sauce

4 servings

Cut thin lengthwise slice from each zucchini. Scoop out centers, leaving ¼-inch shells. Set shells aside.

Crumble sausage into 1-quart casserole. Add onion. Microwave at
High for 4½ to 6½ minutes, or until sausage is no longer pink, stirring
2 or 3 times to break apart. Drain. Stir in stuffing mix. Spoon sausage
mixture evenly into zucchini shells.

Spread rice in even layer on 10 to 12-inch platter. Arrange stuffed zucchini over rice. Spoon 1 tablespoon salsa evenly over top of each
squash. If desired, drizzle additional salsa over rice. Cover with wax
paper. Microwave at 70% (Medium High) for 10 to 15 minutes, or until
stuffing is hot, rotating platter once or twice.

Pepperoni & Provolone Polenta

2⅓ cups hot water
1 teaspoon dried parsley flakes
1 teaspoon instant chicken bouillon granules
½ teaspoon salt
½ teaspoon dried basil leaves
Dash pepper
1 cup yellow cornmeal
¼ cup grated Parmesan cheese
¼ cup butter or margarine, cut up
1 can (16 oz.) whole tomatoes, chopped and drained
¼ teaspoon dried marjoram leaves
½ to ⅔ cup cubed pepperoni (about 3 oz., ¼-inch cubes)
4 slices Provolone cheese
Parmesan cheese (optional)

4 to 8 servings

In 2-quart casserole, combine water, parsley, bouillon, salt, basil and pepper. Cover. Microwave at High for 8 to 10 minutes, or until mixture boils. Using wire whisk, blend in cornmeal, Parmesan cheese and butter. Whisk until butter melts. Microwave, uncovered, at High for 3 to 6 minutes, or until mixture is very thick, stirring once or twice.

Pour mixture in even layer onto 12-inch round platter. Spoon tomatoes evenly over polenta. Sprinkle with marjoram and top with pepperoni. Arrange Provolone cheese in single layer over polenta. Sprinkle with Parmesan. Microwave at 70% (Medium High) for 5 to 7 minutes, or until Provolone cheese melts, rotating platter once or twice.

Italian Peppered Potatoes & Sausages ▲

3 red potatoes (8 to 10 oz. each)
½ cup julienne green pepper (1½ × ¼-inch strips)
½ cup julienne red pepper (1½ × ¼-inch strips)
½ cup julienne yellow pepper (1½ × ¼-inch strips)
2 tablespoons olive oil
1 tablespoon grated Parmesan cheese
½ teaspoon Italian seasoning
¼ teaspoon dried crushed red pepper
¼ teaspoon salt
⅛ teaspoon garlic powder
1 pkg. (16 oz.) fully cooked Polish sausages

4 to 6 servings

Wrap each potato in paper towel. Microwave at High for 10 to 15 minutes, or just until potatoes feel soft, turning over and rearranging once. Let stand for 5 minutes. In medium mixing bowl, combine remaining ingredients, except Polish sausages.

Cut potatoes into ¼-inch slices. Arrange slices in even layer on 12-inch round platter. Top evenly with peppers. Arrange sausages over peppers. Microwave at High for 6 to 10 minutes, or until sausages are hot, rotating platter and rearranging sausages once or twice.

Herbed Chicken Dinner

- 2 cups hot water
- ¾ cup uncooked long-grain white rice
- ½ teaspoon instant chicken bouillon granules
- ½ teaspoon salt
- ⅛ teaspoon dried thyme leaves
- ¼ cup sliced almonds
- 2 tablespoons grated Parmesan cheese
- 1 teaspoon dried parsley flakes
- 1 cup julienne carrot (2½ × ¼-inch strips)
- 2 small zucchini, cut into 1-inch slices
- 1 tablespoon water
- 2 boneless whole chicken breasts (8 to 10 oz. each) cut into halves, skin removed
- ½ teaspoon dried basil leaves

4 servings

How to Microwave Herbed Chicken Dinner

Line four 6-oz. custard cups with plastic wrap. Set aside. In 2-quart casserole, combine hot water, rice, bouillon, salt and thyme. Cover. Microwave at High for 5 minutes. Microwave at 50% (Medium) for 10 to 15 minutes longer, or until rice is tender, stirring once. (Rice will be sticky.)

Stir in almonds, Parmesan and parsley. Spoon mixture evenly into prepared custard cups, packing firmly with spoon. Set aside. Place carrots and zucchini in center of 12-inch round platter. Sprinkle with 1 tablespoon water.

Tuck thin ends under each chicken breast half. Arrange chicken pieces symmetrically around outside edges of platter. Sprinkle chicken with basil and with paprika, if desired. Cover with vented plastic wrap.

Microwave at High for 5 to 9 minutes, or until chicken is firm and no longer pink in center, rotating platter once or twice. Drain through vent in plastic wrap. Set aside.

Microwave rice mixture in custard cups at High for 1 to 3 minutes, or until hot. Remove molded rice from cups and arrange between chicken pieces.

Cornish Hen & Vegetable Platter

2 Cornish game hens
  (18 oz. each)
1 tablespoon butter or
  margarine
3 tablespoons seasoned dry
  bread crumbs
2 tablespoons Italian dressing
¼ teaspoon brown bouquet
  sauce
1 medium red pepper, cut into
  1½-inch chunks
1 medium green pepper, cut
  into 1½-inch chunks
1 medium yellow squash, cut
  into 1½-inch chunks
1 small onion, cut into 8 wedges
2 tablespoons butter or
  margarine, cut up

2 servings

Gently lift and loosen skin from breast area of each Cornish hen. Set aside. In small bowl, microwave butter at High for 45 seconds to 1 minute, or until melted. Add bread crumbs, stirring to coat. Place stuffing mixture under loosened skin of hens. Secure legs together with string. Place hens breast-sides-up on 12-inch round platter. Set aside.

In small bowl, combine Italian dressing and bouquet sauce. Mix well. Brush hens lightly with mixture. Microwave hens at High for 17 to 20 minutes, or until legs move freely and juices run clear, rearranging hens once or twice, and brushing with glaze after half the time. If desired, blot platter with paper towels to absorb cooking liquids. Cover hens with foil and set aside.

Combine remaining ingredients in 1½-quart casserole. Cover and microwave at High for 6 to 7 minutes, or until vegetables are tender-crisp, stirring once. To serve, arrange vegetables around Cornish hens.

Oriental Fish & Peapods

¾ lb. fish fillets (¼ inch thick),
    cut into serving-size pieces
1 cup fresh peapods
1 small onion, cut into 8 pieces,
    separated
2 tablespoons soy sauce
2 teaspoons vegetable oil
1 teaspoon packed brown
    sugar
⅛ teaspoon cayenne
2 radishes, thinly sliced
4 lemon wedges

4 servings

Arrange fish on 12-inch round
platter. Set aside.

Cut decorative notch from stem
end of each peapod. Top fish with
peapods and onion pieces. Set
platter aside.

In 1-cup measure, combine soy
sauce, oil, brown sugar and
cayenne. Mix well. Pour mixture
evenly over fish and vegetables.
Cover with vented plastic wrap.
Microwave at High for 5 to 8 minutes, or until fish is opaque and
flakes easily with a fork. Let stand
for 1 to 2 minutes. Drain through
vent in plastic wrap. Top with
radishes. Arrange lemon wedges
on platter before serving fish.

Baked Stuffed Sole

¼ cup finely chopped celery
¼ cup finely chopped carrot
¼ cup butter or margarine, divided
½ teaspoon grated lemon peel
¼ teaspoon salt
⅛ teaspoon pepper
1 can (6¾ oz.) skinless, boneless salmon, drained
2 tablespoons mayonnaise
1 teaspoon prepared mustard
2 whole sole fillets (about 1 lb. each, ½ to ¾ inch thick)
1 pkg. (10 oz.) frozen peas and carrots
¼ teaspoon paprika
4 to 6 thin slices lemon

4 to 6 servings

How to Microwave Baked Stuffed Sole

Combine celery, carrot, 1 table-spoon butter, the lemon peel, salt and pepper in 1-quart casserole. Cover. Microwave at High for 2½ to 3½ minutes, or until vegetables are tender-crisp, stirring once during cooking time. Add salmon, mayonnaise and mustard. Mix well.

Place one sole fillet in center of 12-inch platter. Top with salmon mixture, spreading to within ½ inch of edge of fillet. Top with remaining fillet.

Cover with wax paper. Microwave at 70% (Medium High) for 13 to 20 minutes, or until fish flakes easily with fork, rotating platter 2 or 3 times. Set aside.

Place frozen vegetables in 1-quart casserole. Cover and microwave at High for 4 to 6 minutes, or until hot, stirring once. Spoon hot vegetables along one side of stuffed sole. Set aside.

Microwave remaining 3 tablespoons butter in small bowl, at High for 1 to 1¼ minutes, or until melted. Stir in paprika. Drizzle fish and vegetables with butter mixture. If desired, microwave platter at 70% (Medium High) for 1 to 2 minutes longer to reheat. Garnish with lemon slices.

Caramel Fruit Platter

1 can (8 oz.) pineapple chunks
1 medium apple, cut into chunks
1 banana, cut into chunks
1 pear, cut into chunks
1 dozen strawberries
1 pkg. (14 oz.) caramels
¼ cup half-and-half

6 servings

Combine fruit in medium bowl. Toss to coat with pineapple juice. Drain. Set aside. Arrange caramels in even layer in center of 12-inch round platter. Pour half-and-half over caramels. Microwave at High for 3½ to 5 minutes, or until caramels melt and mixture can be stirred smooth, stirring 3 or 4 times using a fork.

Arrange fruit around outside edges of platter. Serve fruit platter warm with wooden picks for dipping fruit in caramel.

112

Cherry Cheese Roll

1 cup ricotta cheese
1 egg
2 tablespoons powdered sugar
¼ teaspoon almond extract
¼ cup sliced almonds
1 round sheet lefse (about 12-inch)
1 cup cherry pie filling
Sliced almonds (optional)

4 servings

In small mixing bowl, blend ricotta cheese, egg, powdered sugar and almond extract. Stir in almonds. Spread mixture evenly down center of lefse.

Fold in opposite sides of lefse to enclose filling. Place roll on 12-inch platter.

Microwave at 50% (Medium) for 7 to 11 minutes, or until center of roll is hot, rotating platter once or twice. Top with pie filling. Microwave at High for 1 to 2½ minutes, or until pie filling is hot. Top cheese roll with sliced almonds.

Deluxe Truffles

Melting Chocolate

The secret of successfully melting chocolate is to microwave chocolate at 50% (Medium) and stir often. Without stirring, fully melted chocolate holds its shape and may not look melted. To avoid overheating, microwave just until the last small pieces can be stirred smooth.

The chart below is for candy coating. Some recipes call for other forms of chocolate. Be sure you use the type specified.

For dipping candies, melt chocolate in a measuring cup. Melt it in a mixing bowl when additional ingredients are to be stirred in.

Cool chocolate-dipped candies on a baking sheet lined with wax paper, or on a rack set over wax paper to catch the drips.

Stir cereal, nuts or pretzels into leftover melted candy coating to make quick crunches. Spread mixture on wax paper, cool and break into pieces.

Make truffles on a cool day and work quickly so heat from your hands doesn't melt the rich mixture.

Candy Coating Melting Chart

Amount	Container	Method	Microwave at 50% (Medium)
¼ lb., broken into squares	Small mixing bowl, or 2-cup measure	Place candy coating and 1 teaspoon to 2 tablespoons shortening in container. Microwave until coating can be stirred smooth, stirring once or twice.	2 to 4 min.
½ lb., broken into squares			2½ to 5 min.
¾ lb., broken into squares	Medium mixing bowl, or 1-quart measure	Place candy coating and 1 to 2 tablespoons shortening in container. Microwave until coating can be stirred smooth, stirring once or twice.	2½ to 5½ min.
1 lb., broken into squares			4 to 8 min.

Chocolate Wafer Creams

Line a baking sheet with wax paper and set aside. In 1-quart measure, combine ½ lb. white or chocolate-flavored candy coating and 1 tablespoon shortening. Microwave as directed in chart (opposite), or until mixture is melted. Using a fork, dip 2 dozen cream-filled wafers to coat. Place cookies on prepared baking sheet, and let cool until set. Store wafer creams in airtight container or plastic food-storage bag. Yields 2 dozen wafers.

Chocolate-covered Pudding or Gelatin Pops

Line a baking sheet with wax paper and set aside. In 1-quart measure, place ½ lb. white or chocolate-flavored candy coating and 1 to 2 tablespoons shortening. Microwave as directed in chart (opposite), or until melted. Dip a frozen pudding or gelatin bar (1.75 to 1.8 oz. each) in coating. If desired, quickly coat with colored or chocolate shot. Hold bar a few seconds to allow coating to set. Place bar on prepared baking sheet in freezer. Wrap coated bars in plastic wrap to store in freezer. Yields 12 coated bars.

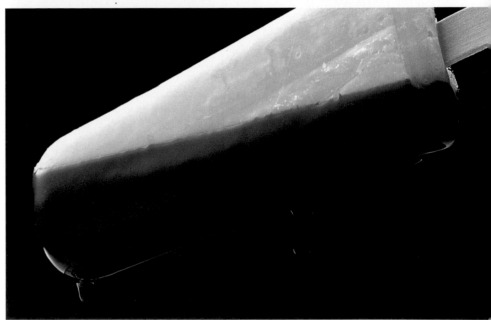

All-American Kids' Treats

Count out forty 100% whole wheat wafers from 9½-oz. box. Spread 20 of the crackers with peanut butter. Spread the rest of the crackers with your favorite jam, jelly or preserves. Sandwich the peanut butter and jam sides together. Line a baking sheet with wax paper and set aside.

In 2-cup measure, place ½ lb. chocolate-flavored candy coating and 1 tablespoon shortening. Microwave as directed in chart (opposite), or until melted. Using 2 forks, dip each sandwich into melted chocolate to coat. Place treats on prepared baking sheet, and chill until set. Store treats in airtight container or plastic food-storage bag. Yields 20 treats.

How to Microwave Chocolate-covered Cherries

Chocolate-covered ▲ Cherries

¼ cup butter or margarine
2 cups powdered sugar
¼ cup sweetened condensed milk
36 maraschino cherries
1 lb. chocolate-flavored candy coating, broken into squares
1 tablespoon shortening

3 dozen cherries

Place butter in medium mixing bowl. Microwave at 30% (Medium Low) for 15 to 45 seconds, or until softened, checking after every 15 seconds. Add powdered sugar. Mix well. Blend in condensed milk. (Mixture will be stiff.)

Cover each cherry with about 1 teaspoon sugar mixture. (For easy handling, coat hands with powdered sugar.) Place cherries on wax-paper-lined baking sheet. Chill cherries for 30 minutes.

Combine chocolate and shortening in 1-quart casserole. Microwave at 50% (Medium) for 5 to 8 minutes, or until the mixture can be stirred smooth, stirring once or twice.

Dip coated cherries in chocolate using two forks. Place on prepared baking sheet and chill until set. (If necessary, microwave chocolate at 50% (Medium) for 1 to 3 minutes, or until remelted.)

Redip cherries in chocolate. Let cherries cool until chocolate sets. Cover loosely with wax paper. Set aside in cool place for 2 to 3 days to allow centers to soften.

Chocolate Apricot Chews ▲

1 pkg. (3 oz.) cream cheese
1 tablespoon powdered sugar
¼ teaspoon vanilla
1 pkg. (6 oz.) dried apricot
   halves

1 pkg. (6 oz.) semisweet
   chocolate chips
1 tablespoon shortening

About 15 candies

In small bowl, microwave cream cheese at High for 15 to 30 seconds, or until softened. Add powdered sugar and vanilla. Mix well. Place small amount of cream cheese mixture between two apricot halves. Press halves together lightly. Repeat with remaining apricot halves and cream cheese mixture. Arrange stuffed apricots on plate. Chill for 15 minutes, or until cream cheese filling is firm. Line a baking sheet with wax paper and set aside.

In small mixing bowl, combine chocolate chips and shortening. Microwave at 50% (Medium) for 3½ to 4½ minutes, or until chocolate is glossy and mixture can be stirred smooth, stirring once or twice. Using two forks, dip stuffed apricots into chocolate mixture, turning to coat completely. Or dip one half only. Arrange apricots on prepared baking sheet. Chill for 15 to 20 minutes, or until chocolate is set. Serve chilled.

Caramel Pecan Clusters ▲

Remove wrappers from 12 caramels. Set aside. Line a baking sheet with wax paper and set aside. In small mixing bowl, combine ¼ lb. chocolate-flavored candy coating and 1 teaspoon shortening. Microwave as directed in chart (page 116), or until mixture melts. Stir in 2 tablespoons finely chopped pecans. With spoon, dip each caramel into chocolate mixture to coat. Drop dipped caramels onto prepared baking sheet. Let clusters cool until set. Store in airtight container or plastic food-storage bag.

Yields 12 clusters

Chocolate Chews

2 squares (1 oz. each)
   unsweetened chocolate
2 tablespoons butter or
   margarine
⅓ cup light corn syrup
½ teaspoon vanilla
2 cups powdered sugar,
   divided
½ cup non-fat dry milk powder

1¼ lbs.

In medium mixing bowl, combine chocolate and butter. Microwave at 50% (Medium) for 3 to 4½ minutes, or until chocolate is glossy and mixture can be stirred smooth, stirring once or twice. Blend in corn syrup and vanilla. Microwave at High for 1 minute.

Mix in 1¾ cups powdered sugar and the dry milk powder. Spread remaining ¼ cup powdered sugar on wooden board. Turn chocolate out onto sugared board and knead until extra sugar is absorbed. Divide dough into 8 equal portions. Roll each portion into ½-inch diameter rope. Cut each piece into 1½-inch lengths. Let chocolate chews cool. Wrap each in wax paper.

Candy Pizza

1 recipe pizza base (right)
2 cups stir-ins (right)
½ to ¾ cup toppings (right)
1 recipe frosting (right)

1½ lbs.

How to Make Candy Pizza

Line baking sheet with wax or parchment paper. Set aside. Microwave candy pizza base. Add combined choice of stir-ins. Mix well to coat.

Spread base mixture evenly on prepared baking sheet to 10-inch diameter. Sprinkle with combined choice of toppings. Set aside.

Microwave frosting. Drizzle frosting over candy pizza. Chill for at least 1½ hours, or until set. Peel off wax paper. Break candy apart, or serve in wedges.

Candy Pizza Base

Light Chocolate:
In medium mixing bowl, combine 1½ cups milk chocolate chips and 3 squares (1 oz. each) semisweet chocolate. Microwave at 50% (Medium) for 4 to 6 minutes, or until chocolate can be stirred smooth, stirring twice.

White Chocolate:
In medium mixing bowl, combine ¾ lb. white candy coating (broken into squares) and 1 tablespoon shortening. Microwave at 50% (Medium) for 2½ to 5½ minutes, or until mixture can be stirred smooth, stirring twice.

Peanut Butter:
In medium mixing bowl, combine 1½ cups peanut butter chips and 3 oz. white candy coating. Microwave at 50% (Medium) for 4 to 6 minutes, or until mixture can be stirred smooth, stirring twice.

Dark Chocolate:
In medium mixing bowl, combine 1½ cups semisweet chocolate chips and 3 squares (1 oz. each) unsweetened chocolate. Microwave at 50% (Medium) for 4 to 6 minutes, or until chocolate can be stirred smooth, stirring twice.

Mint Chocolate:
In medium mixing bowl, combine 1½ cups mint-flavored semisweet chocolate chips and 3 squares (1 oz. each) semisweet chocolate. Microwave at 50% (Medium) for 4 to 6 minutes, or until chocolate can be stirred smooth, stirring once or twice.

Butterscotch:
In medium mixing bowl, combine 1½ cups butterscotch chips and 3 oz. white candy coating. Microwave at 50% (Medium) for 4 to 6 minutes, or until mixture can be stirred smooth, stirring twice.

Candy Pizza Stir-ins

Use one or more of the following, to equal 2 cups:

Crisp rice cereal
Toasted round oat cereal
Corn flakes cereal
Crisp square rice, wheat or corn cereal
Coarsely crushed pretzel sticks
Coarsely crushed shoestring potatoes
Salted mixed nuts
Chopped nuts
Salted dry-roasted peanuts
Whole or slivered almonds
Miniature marshmallows

Candy Pizza Frosting

¼ lb. white or chocolate-flavored candy coating

Candy Pizza Toppings

Use one or more of the following toppings, to equal ½ to ¾ cup:

Miniature jelly beans
Jellied orange slices, cut up
Candied fruit
Candied cherries, cut up
Maraschino cherries, drained
Red or black licorice pieces
Shredded coconut
Candy-coated plain or peanut chocolate pieces
Candy-coated peanut butter pieces
Chocolate-covered raisins
Candy corn

1 teaspoon shortening

Frosts one candy pizza

In 2-cup measure, combine candy coating and shortening. Microwave as directed in chart (page 116), or until melted. Drizzle frosting over candy pizza.

Basic Truffles

2 bars (4 oz. each) sweet baking
    chocolate, cut up
⅓ cup whipping cream
3 tablespoons butter or
    margarine
½ teaspoon vanilla

Coatings:
    Powdered sugar
    Cocoa
    Finely chopped nuts
    Shredded coconut

24 truffles

Line an 8 × 4-inch loaf dish with plastic wrap. Set aside. In 1-quart measure, combine chocolate, whipping cream and butter. Microwave at 50% (Medium) for 4 to 6 minutes, or until chocolate melts and mixture can be stirred smooth, stirring once. Beat mixture until smooth and shiny. Blend in vanilla. Pour mixture into prepared loaf dish. Refrigerate for 4 hours. Lift chocolate mixture from dish and cut into 24 equal portions. Let stand for 10 minutes.

Coat hands lightly with powdered sugar and roll each portion into ¾-inch ball. Place desired coating in small bowl and roll each ball to coat. Place each truffle in paper candy cup and chill for at least 1 hour before serving. Store truffles in refrigerator for no longer than 2 weeks.

Variation: Follow recipe above, except omit vanilla and substitute another complementary flavored extract (maple, almond, cherry, orange, peppermint, etc.).

TIP: Work quickly when rolling mixture into balls. Chocolate mixture is rich, and melts easily.

◄ Deluxe Truffles

2 bars (4 oz. each) sweet baking chocolate, cut up
⅓ cup whipping cream
3 tablespoons butter or margarine
1 tablespoon liqueur (almond, cherry, orange, etc.)

Coating:
½ lb. white or chocolate-flavored candy coating, divided
¼ cup shortening, divided

Decoration:
1 square (1 oz.) semisweet chocolate
1 teaspoon shortening

10 truffles

TIP: For pastel-colored truffles, or decorative toppings, tint white candy coating with 1 or 2 drops food coloring.

How to Microwave Deluxe Truffles

Line an 8 × 4-inch loaf dish with plastic wrap. Set aside. In 1-quart measure, combine chocolate, whipping cream and butter. Microwave at 50% (Medium) for 4 to 6 minutes, or until chocolate melts and mixture can be stirred smooth, stirring once. Beat until smooth and shiny. Blend in liqueur. Pour into prepared loaf dish. Refrigerate for 4 hours.

Lift chocolate mixture from dish and cut into 10 equal portions. Let stand for 10 minutes. Line a baking sheet with wax paper and set aside. Coat hands lightly with powdered sugar and roll each portion into 1¼-inch ball. Place on prepared baking sheet. Chill for 15 minutes.

Combine ¼ lb. candy coating and 2 tablespoons shortening in 2-cup measure. Microwave as directed in chart (page 116), or until mixture melts. Using fork, dip each chocolate ball in candy coating. Place on prepared baking sheet. Chill until set.

Combine remaining candy coating and shortening in clean 2-cup measure. Microwave as directed in chart (page 116), or until melted. Redip truffles and chill until coating is set.

Place semisweet chocolate square and 1 teaspoon shortening in small bowl. Microwave at 50% (Medium) for 2½ to 4½ minutes, or until chocolate is glossy and mixture can be stirred smooth, stirring once. Drizzle melted chocolate in decorative design over tops of coated truffles. Chill before serving. Store truffles in refrigerator for no longer than 2 weeks.

How to Microwave Monster Cookies

Monster Cookies

¾ cup shortening
1 cup packed brown sugar
1 egg
¼ cup water
1 teaspoon vanilla
3 cups rolled oats
1 cup all-purpose flour
¾ teaspoon salt
½ teaspoon baking soda
1 cup butterscotch chips or
   candy-coated plain
   chocolate pieces
½ cup chopped nuts

5 cookies

Combine shortening, brown sugar, egg, water and vanilla in large mixing bowl. Beat at medium speed of electric mixer until mixture is light and fluffy.

Add oats, flour, salt and baking soda. Mix well. Stir in butterscotch chips and nuts.

Divide dough into 5 equal portions (about 1 cup dough for each). On wax-paper-lined plate, pat one portion into ½-inch thickness (diameter will be 5½ to 6 inches).

Microwave cookie at 70% (Medium High) for 3 to 5 minutes, or just until dry on surface, rotating plate once.

Press extra chips or candies into top of cookie, if desired. Let cookie stand on counter until cool. Repeat with remaining dough.

Quick Pastry Cookies

1 cup all-purpose flour
¼ cup finely chopped pecans
2 tablespoons sugar
1 teaspoon grated orange peel
¼ teaspoon salt
¼ cup shortening
3 tablespoons butter or
   margarine, cut up
2 tablespoons cold water
1 teaspoon vanilla

Frosting:
¾ cup semisweet chocolate
   chips
1 teaspoon shortening

16 cookies

In medium mixing bowl, combine flour, pecans, sugar, orange peel and salt. Cut in shortening and butter until particles resemble coarse crumbs. In small bowl, mix water and vanilla. Sprinkle mixture over dough, stirring with fork until particles are just moist enough to cling together and form ball. (Use additional 1 teaspoon water, if necessary.)

Divide dough into 2 equal portions. Between sheets of wax paper, roll out one portion to ¼-inch thickness. Using cookie cutter, cut out eight 2-inch rounds. Arrange cut-outs in circle around edge of wax-paper-lined plate. Microwave cookies at High for 2 to 3 minutes, or until dry and puffy, rotating plate once or twice. Place cookies on cooling rack. (Cookies crisp as they cool.) Repeat with remaining dough. Cool cookies completely.

In 1-cup measure, combine frosting ingredients. Microwave at 50% (Medium) for 2½ to 3½ minutes, or until chocolate is glossy and can be stirred smooth, stirring once. Dip half of each cooled cookie into chocolate. Return cookies to rack until chocolate sets.

How to Microwave Ice Cream Sandwiches

Ice Cream Sandwiches

1 cup all-purpose flour
¼ teaspoon baking soda
¼ cup shortening
¼ cup sugar
1 egg
½ teaspoon vanilla
4 squares (1 oz. each) semisweet chocolate
1 square carton (½ gallon) ice cream

4 servings

TIP: Serve sandwiches immediately, or wrap in aluminum foil and store in freezer.

Combine flour and baking soda in small bowl. Mix well and set aside. In medium mixing bowl, combine shortening and sugar. Beat at medium speed of electric mixer until mixture is light and fluffy. Add egg and vanilla. Beat until mixture is smooth. Set aside.

Place chocolate in 2-cup measure, microwave at 50% (Medium) for 2½ to 4½ minutes, or until chocolate is glossy and can be stirred smooth, stirring once or twice. Blend into egg mixture. Add flour mixture. Mix well. Shape dough into a ball, flattening slightly. Wrap in plastic wrap and chill for about 15 minutes, or until firm.

Roll out dough to ¼-inch thickness between sheets of wax paper. Using a 3-inch round biscuit or cookie cutter, cut out 8 rounds. Arrange 4 rounds on wax-paper-lined plate. Prick each round several times with fork.

Microwave chocolate rounds at High for 2 to 2½ minutes, or just until surfaces appear dry and slightly puffed, rotating plate every 30 seconds. Let rounds cool slightly before removing from wax paper. Repeat with remaining rounds.

Open one end of ice cream carton. Cut four 1-inch slices from ice cream. (Refreeze remaining ice cream.) Lay ice cream slices on wax paper. Cut four 3-inch rounds. Place each ice cream round between 2 chocolate rounds to make four sandwiches.

127

Light Yogurt Freeze Pops

1⅔ cups cold water, divided
  1 pkg. (0.3 oz.) low-calorie
      strawberry gelatin
  1 pkg. (16 oz.) frozen
      unsweetened strawberries
1⅓ cups plain low-fat yogurt
  2 tablespoons honey

6 pops

In 2-cup measure, microwave 1 cup water at High for 2 to 3 minutes, or until boiling. Add gelatin, stirring thoroughly to dissolve. Stir in remaining ⅔ cup cold water. Set aside.

In large mixing bowl, microwave strawberries at 50% (Medium) for 5 to 7 minutes, or until defrosted but still very cold, stirring once. Stir in yogurt and honey. Blend in gelatin mixture. Freeze for about 1½ hours, or until mixture is slushy. With electric mixer, beat yogurt mixture until smooth.

Spoon mixture evenly into six 7-oz. wax-coated paper cups. Insert flat sticks in center of each filled cup. Freeze for about 5 hours, or until pops are firm.

TIP: To serve pudding and gelatin pops, run bottoms of cups under warm water to loosen pops.

Frozen Pudding Treats

1 pkg. (3 oz.) vanilla pudding and pie filling
2 cups milk
½ cup semisweet or milk chocolate chips
½ cup butterscotch chips
2 cups non-dairy whipped topping

6 pops

Place pudding mix in 1-quart measure. Blend in milk. Microwave at High for 6 to 9 minutes, or until mixture boils, stirring with whisk after every 2 minutes.

Pour one-half of the pudding into small mixing bowl. Add chocolate chips to one portion. Add butterscotch chips to second portion. Stir each mixture smooth. Place plastic wrap directly on pudding surface of each portion and chill for 1 hour.

Blend 1 cup whipped topping into each pudding. Alternate layers of chocolate and butterscotch mixtures evenly filling six 7-oz. wax-coated paper cups.

Insert flat wooden stick in center of each filled pudding cup. Freeze for about 6 hours, or until firm.

Orange-Pineapple Freezer Pops

1 cup cold water, divided
1 teaspoon unflavored gelatin
1 can (8 oz.) crushed pineapple in heavy syrup (undrained)
1 can (6 oz.) frozen orange juice concentrate

6 pops

Place ½ cup water in 1-quart measure. Sprinkle with gelatin. Let stand for 5 minutes to soften. Microwave at High for 30 seconds to 1 minute, or until gelatin dissolves. Set aside.

In food processor or blender, purée pineapple. Add pineapple and remaining ½ cup water to gelatin mixture. Set aside. Remove lid from frozen juice concentrate. Microwave at High for 30 seconds to 1½ minutes, or until juice defrosts. Mix juice into pineapple mixture. Pour mixture evenly into six 5-oz. wax-coated paper cups. Freeze for 1½ hours. Insert flat stick in center of each cup. Freeze for about 4 hours, or until firm.

Apple Freezer Pops: Follow recipe above, except substitute 1 cup applesauce for the puréed pineapple and 1 can (6 oz.) frozen apple juice concentrate for the orange juice.

Fruit-flavored Popcorn Bars

1 bag (10 oz.) large
   marshmallows
¼ cup butter or margarine,
   cut up
3 tablespoons fruit-flavored
   gelatin powder (any flavor)
8 cups popped popcorn
½ cup dry-roasted peanuts
   (optional)

16 popcorn bars

How to Microwave Fruit-flavored Popcorn Bars

Grease 9-inch square baking
dish. Set aside. In large mixing
bowl, place marshmallows and
butter. Microwave at High for 2 to
3 minutes, or until marshmallows
puff and mixture can be stirred
smooth, stirring 2 or 3 times.

Add gelatin. Mix well. Add popcorn and peanuts. Stir to coat.
With buttered fingers, press
popcorn mixture into prepared
baking dish. Let mixture cool, and
cut into 16 bars.

**Fruit-flavored Popcorn
Sculptures:** Follow recipe above,
except shape popcorn mixture
into any desired shape on greased
baking sheet.

Red Hot Popcorn Balls

¼ cup plus 2 tablespoons butter
   or margarine
½ cup red cinnamon candies
10 large marshmallows
⅓ cup packed brown sugar
2 tablespoons light corn syrup
8 cups popped popcorn

6 popcorn balls

In large mixing bowl, combine butter and cinnamon candies. Microwave at High for 3½ to 4 minutes, or until candies are melted and can be stirred smooth. Add marshmallows, brown sugar and corn syrup. Microwave at High for 1 to 1½ minutes, or until marshmallows puff and mixture can be stirred smooth, stirring 2 or 3 times. Add popcorn. Stir to coat.

With buttered fingers, shape popcorn mixture into 6 balls. Let popcorn balls cool. Wrap with plastic wrap, and tie with ribbon, if desired.

Popcorn Sculptures: Follow recipe above, except shape prepared popcorn mixture into any desired shape on greased baking sheet. Decorate with prepared frosting, jelly beans or decorator sprinkles.

Sit-down Sweets

For the finale of an elegant dinner, or as the centerpiece of a dessert-and-coffee party, or to make any occasion special, try one of these spectacular sweets. Microwave cooking simplifies traditional procedures, like scalding milk, heating softened gelatin, melting chocolate, softening cream cheese or ice cream, or even toasting coconut. It eliminates some time-consuming techniques completely. Delicate egg and milk desserts stay smooth without constant stirring, and microwaving allows you to omit water-bath cooking methods often used to prevent toughening.

Floating Island ▶

```
 4  eggs, separated
⅔  cup sugar, divided
 2  cups milk
 1  tablespoon all-purpose flour
½  teaspoon vanilla
```

4 servings

How to Microwave Floating Island

Place egg whites in large mixing bowl. Reserve yolks in medium mixing bowl. At high speed of electric mixer, beat egg whites until soft peaks form. Gradually add ⅓ cup sugar while continuing to beat at high speed. Set meringue mixture aside.

Pour milk and remaining ⅓ cup sugar into 10-inch square casserole. Cover, and microwave at High for 5 to 8 minutes, or until sugar is dissolved and milk is steaming but not boiling, stirring once or twice.

Scoop out one-fourth of the meringue mixture using 2 large spoons, and drop into steaming milk. Repeat to yield 4 servings. Cover, and microwave at 50% (Medium) for 3 to 5 minutes, or just until meringue feels firm, rotating dish once.

Ginger Caramel Custard

2 cups half-and-half
⅓ cup packed brown sugar
1 tablespoon finely chopped
   crystallized ginger
½ teaspoon vanilla
3 egg yolks, beaten

4 servings

In 1½-quart casserole, combine half-and-half, brown sugar and ginger. Mix well. Microwave at High for 3 to 5 minutes, or until mixture is hot but not boiling, stirring once or twice. Stir in vanilla. Gradually stir small amount of hot mixture into egg yolks. Blend egg yolks back into hot mixture.

Divide mixture evenly between four 6-oz. custard cups. Arrange cups in circular pattern in oven. Microwave at 50% (Medium) for 5 to 9 minutes, or until custard is soft-set, rearranging 3 times. Chill before serving. Garnish servings with whipped cream and additional chopped, crystallized ginger, if desired.

Remove meringues with slotted spatula and place on paper-towel-lined baking sheet. Chill. Blend flour and vanilla into egg yolks. Mix well. Gradually stir small amount of hot milk mixture into egg yolk mixture.

Blend in remaining milk mixture. Microwave at 50% (Medium) for 6 to 10 minutes, or until custard thickens enough to coat back of metal spoon, stirring after every minute.

Pour custard evenly into 4 serving dishes. Using spatula, carefully lift meringues from paper towel and place in serving dishes. Meringues should float on surface of custard. Serve immediately.

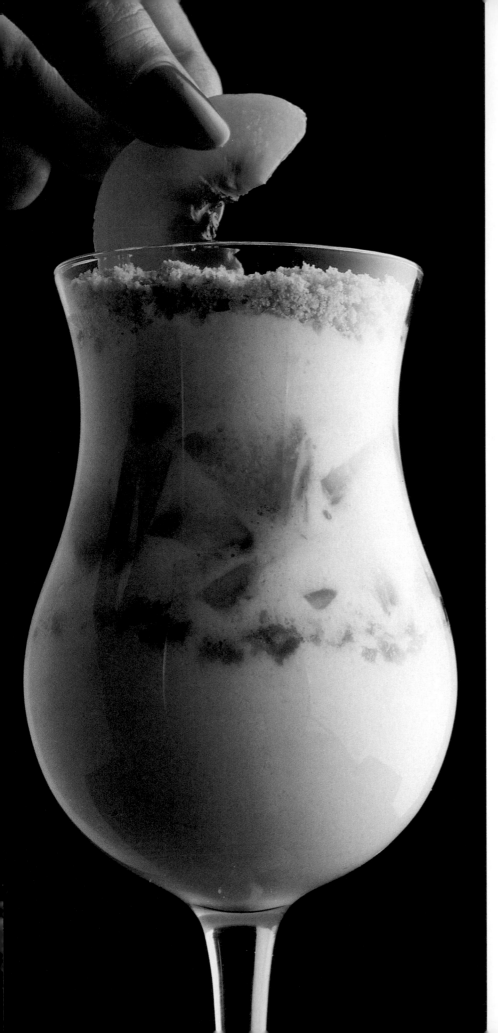

Peachy Orange Parfait

½ cup milk
⅓ cup sugar
2 egg yolks
½ teaspoon cornstarch
1 cup orange juice
1 teaspoon unflavored gelatin
1 cup prepared whipped topping
2 cups frozen sliced peaches
1 cup coarsely crushed vanilla
   wafer crumbs

4 servings

In 1-cup measure, microwave milk at High for 1¼ to 1½ minutes, or until scalded. Set aside. In medium mixing bowl, combine sugar, egg yolks and cornstarch. Mix well. Gradually blend hot milk into sugar mixture. Microwave at 50% (Medium) for 4 to 6 minutes, or until custard thickens enough to coat back of metal spoon, stirring after every minute. Chill.

Place orange juice in 2-cup measure. Sprinkle gelatin over orange juice. Let stand for 5 minutes to soften. Microwave at High for 1 to 1½ minutes, or until mixture is hot and gelatin is dissolved, stirring once. Chill for about 1½ hours, or until soft-set. Blend gelatin into custard. Fold in whipped topping.

In small mixing bowl, microwave frozen peaches at 50% (Medium) for 3 to 5 minutes, or until defrosted, stirring once. Chop peaches and set aside. In each of 4 individual parfait glasses or sherbet dishes, layer ingredients in the following order: orange juice mixture, wafer crumbs, peaches, orange juice mixture and wafer crumbs. Chill parfaits for about 2 hours, or until orange layers are firm.

Lemon Custard Pudding ▶

½ cup sugar
2 tablespoons cornstarch
1 tablespoon all-purpose flour
1 teaspoon grated lemon peel
¼ teaspoon salt
1 cup milk
1 cup half-and-half
2 egg yolks, beaten
3 tablespoons lemon juice

4 servings

In medium mixing bowl, combine sugar, cornstarch, flour, lemon peel and salt. Mix well. Blend in milk and half-and-half. Microwave at 70% (Medium High) for 11 to 14 minutes, or until mixture thickens, stirring with whisk 3 or 4 times. Gradually stir small amount of hot milk mixture into egg yolks. Blend egg yolks back into hot mixture. Microwave at 50% (Medium) for 1 to 2 minutes longer, or until custard thickens. Blend in lemon juice.

Place sheet of plastic wrap directly on surface of custard to prevent skin from forming. Chill for at least 3 hours. Garnish with whipped cream or fresh, sliced fruit, if desired.

TIP: Serve pudding over individual shortcakes or a split ladyfinger.

Bourbon Pecan Cream

1 cup sugar, divided
1 tablespoon plus 1½ teaspoons cornstarch
⅛ teaspoon salt
1½ cups half-and-half
4 egg yolks, beaten
3 tablespoons bourbon

2 pkgs. (3 oz. each) cream cheese
¼ cup butter or margarine, softened (page 82)
2 cups finely chopped pecans
Whipped cream
Finely chopped pecans

4 to 6 servings

In medium mixing bowl, mix ½ cup sugar, the cornstarch and salt. Blend in half-and-half. Microwave at High for 5 to 10 minutes, or until mixture is very thick, stirring 2 or 3 times. Gradually stir small amount of hot mixture into egg yolks. Blend egg yolks back into hot mixture. Microwave at High for 1 to 2 minutes longer, or until mixture thickens, stirring with whisk every 30 seconds. Blend in bourbon. Place sheet of plastic wrap directly on surface to prevent skin from forming. Chill for 2 to 3 hours, or until mixture is cool.*

In medium mixing bowl, microwave cream cheese at 50% (Medium) for 1 to 1½ minutes, or until softened. Set aside. Add softened butter and remaining sugar to cream cheese. Using electric mixer, beat until blended. Stir in pecans. Fold in custard mixture. Spoon into dessert dishes. Top with whipped cream, and sprinkle with pecans.

*For faster cooling, place mixing bowl in larger dish containing 1 to 2 inches ice water. Chill both bowls until custard cools.

Caramel Apple Torte ▶

  2 cups all-purpose flour
  2 tablespoons sugar
1½ teaspoons ground cinnamon
  ½ teaspoon salt
  ½ cup shortening
  ¼ cup butter or margarine,
     cut up
  3 to 6 tablespoons cold water
20 caramels
  1 tablespoon milk
  1 can (20 oz.) apple pie filling

6 servings

TIP: For Pastry Circle: Roll dough into circle slightly larger than 7 inches. Use a 7-inch plate as a guide to cut perfect pastry circle.

How to Microwave Caramel Apple Torte

Combine flour, sugar, cinnamon and salt in large mixing bowl. Cut in shortening and butter until particles are size of small peas. Sprinkle water over mixture one tablespoon at a time, mixing with fork, just until particles are moistened enough to cling together. Form mixture into ball. Flatten slightly. Wrap ball in plastic wrap and chill for 15 minutes.

Caribbean Cobbler ▲

½ pkg. (17¼ oz.) frozen puff
   pastry sheets
3 lbs. papayas (about 3 large)
½ cup packed brown sugar
2 tablespoons all-purpose flour

½ teaspoon ground cinnamon
2 tablespoons butter or
   margarine, cut up
2 tablespoons lime juice
½ teaspoon grated lime peel

4 to 6 servings

Heat conventional oven to 400°F. Unfold one pastry sheet on a lightly floured surface. Using cover from 2-quart round casserole as guide, cut circle from pastry sheet. Place circle on baking sheet. Score pastry sheet with decorative designs, if desired. Bake for 10 to 15 minutes, or until puffed and golden brown. Remove pastry from oven and set aside.

Peel each papaya and cut in half lengthwise. Remove seeds. Cut papaya into 1-inch chunks. Set aside. In a 2-quart casserole, combine brown sugar, flour and cinnamon. Mix well. Add papaya, butter, lime juice and lime peel. Stir gently to combine. Cover, and microwave at High for 10 to 16 minutes, or until papaya is very tender, stirring once or twice. Top hot papaya mixture with baked pastry. Serve immediately.

Divide dough into 3 equal portions. On lightly floured surface, roll each portion and cut into 7-inch circle. Transfer each pastry circle to sheet of wax paper. Prick circles generously with fork. Microwave one at a time on wax paper at High for 3 to 4 minutes, or until firm and dry, rotating after every minute.

Cool pastry on wire rack. Remove wax paper. Set pastry aside. Repeat with remaining pastry circles. In medium mixing bowl, combine caramels and milk. Microwave at High for 2 to 2½ minutes, or until caramels are melted and can be stirred smooth, stirring twice.

Place one pastry circle on plate. Top with 2 tablespoons melted caramel, spreading to within ½ inch of edge. Top with one-third of apple pie filling and another pastry circle. Repeat sequence twice. Cut torte into wedges to serve.

137

Carrot Almond Torte ▲

Cake:

½ cup granulated sugar
¼ cup packed brown sugar
3 tablespoons vegetable oil
3 eggs, separated
1 cup finely shredded carrot
2 tablespoons lemon juice
1 teaspoon grated lemon peel
1 cup ground almonds
½ cup all-purpose flour
⅓ cup unseasoned dry
　　bread crumbs
¾ teaspoon baking powder
¾ teaspoon pumpkin pie spice
¼ teaspoon salt

Glaze:

½ cup peach preserves
1 teaspoon lemon juice

Topping:

½ cup whipping cream
1 tablespoon powdered sugar
　Sliced almonds (optional)

8 servings

How to Microwave Carrot Almond Torte

Line bottom of 9-inch round cake dish with wax paper and set aside. In medium mixing bowl, combine sugars, oil and egg yolks. Reserve egg whites. With electric mixer, beat until mixture is light and fluffy. Add remaining cake ingredients. Beat until well mixed. Set aside.

Beat egg whites until stiff peaks form using clean beaters. Fold egg whites into torte mixture. Pour batter into prepared dish. Place on saucer in microwave oven. Microwave at 50% (Medium) for 6 minutes. Rotate dish half turn.

Chocolate Rum Cake

1 pkg. (9 oz.) devil's food
   cake mix

Glaze:
½ cup sugar
¼ cup butter or margarine
⅓ cup dark rum

Frosting:
1⅓ cups whipping cream
2 tablespoons sugar
2 tablespoons dark rum
   (optional)

8 servings

Line bottom of 9-inch square baking dish with wax paper and set aside. Prepare cake mix as directed on package. Pour batter into prepared baking dish. Place dish on saucer in microwave oven. Microwave at 50% (Medium) for 6 minutes. Rotate dish half turn. Microwave at High for 2 to 5 minutes longer, or until top appears dry and center springs back when touched lightly, rotating dish once or twice. Let cake stand on counter for 10 minutes. Pierce cake thoroughly with thin knife and set aside.

In 2-cup measure, combine all glaze ingredients. Microwave at 50% (Medium) for 3 to 4 minutes, or until mixture boils, stirring once or twice. Pour glaze slowly over hot cake. Chill cake for at least 3 hours, or overnight.

Loosen edges and invert cake onto wire rack. Peel off wax paper. Set cake aside. In medium mixing bowl, beat whipping cream until thickened. Gradually add sugar while continuing to beat until mixture is stiff. Fold in rum. Set frosting aside.

Cut cake in half. Place one half on serving plate and top evenly with about 1 cup frosting. Top with remaining cake half. Spread remaining frosting evenly over top and sides. Decorate cake with chocolate shavings and maraschino cherries, if desired. Serve immediately.

Microwave at High for 3 to 6 minutes longer, or until top appears dry and no uncooked batter remains on bottom, rotating dish twice. Let cake stand on counter for 5 minutes. Invert cake onto wire rack. Cool slightly. Place on serving plate.

Combine all glaze ingredients in 1-cup measure. Microwave at High for 1 to 2 minutes, or until mixture is hot and bubbly, stirring once. Spread glaze on top and sides of cake. Cool cake completely.

Beat whipping cream in small mixing bowl until thickened. Gradually add powdered sugar, while continuing to beat until mixture is stiff. Pipe frosting around edge of cake. Decorate top of cake with almonds.

Chocolate Cheese Tarts

1 tablespoon butter or
    margarine
1 tablespoon sugar
½ cup graham cracker crumbs
2 squares (1 oz. each)
    semisweet chocolate
1 pkg. (3 oz.) cream cheese,
    softened (page 84)
2 eggs
2 tablespoons lemon juice
1 can (14 oz.) sweetened
    condensed milk

Toppings:
    Cherry pie filling
    Whipped cream
    Chocolate curls

8 servings

Place 2 paper liners in each of eight 6-oz. custard cups. Set aside. In small bowl, microwave butter at High for 45 seconds to 1 minute, or until melted. Stir in sugar and cracker crumbs. Mix well. Place 1 tablespoon crumb mixture in bottom of each lined custard cup, pressing lightly. Set aside.

In small bowl, microwave chocolate at 50% (Medium) for 2½ to 3½ minutes, or until chocolate is glossy and can be stirred smooth, stirring once or twice. In medium mixing bowl, combine chocolate and softened cream cheese. Mix well. Add eggs, lemon juice and condensed milk. Beat at medium speed of electric mixer until mixture is smooth, scraping bowl frequently.

Spoon chocolate mixture evenly into paper liners. Arrange 4 tarts in microwave oven. Microwave at 50% (Medium) for 4 to 6 minutes, or until tarts are firm and just begin to puff. Repeat with remaining tarts. Chill for 3 to 4 hours. Top tarts with one or more toppings before serving.

How to Microwave White Chocolate Cheesecake

◄ **White Chocolate Cheesecake**

Crust:

⅓ cup butter or margarine
1⅓ cups finely crushed chocolate-covered graham cookie crumbs (about 20 cookies)

Filling:

1 pkg. (8 oz.) cream cheese, softened (page 84)
1⅓ cups ricotta cheese
3 eggs
2 tablespoons cornstarch
2 tablespoons cherry liqueur
½ lb. white chocolate or white candy coating, melted (page 116)

8 to 10 servings

Line 9-inch round cake dish with two 4 × 15-inch strips of parchment paper, crisscrossing strips at bottom. (Ends of paper should hang over edge of dish.)

Place butter in small mixing bowl. Microwave at High for 1½ to 1¾ minutes, or until butter melts. Add cookie crumbs, stirring until moistened. Press crumb mixture onto bottom of prepared cake dish. Set aside.

Combine cream cheese, ricotta, eggs, cornstarch and liqueur in large mixing bowl. With electric mixer, beat until mixture is well blended. Mix in white chocolate.

Pour batter into prepared dish. Microwave at 50% (Medium) for 15 to 20 minutes, or until cheesecake is almost set in center, rotating dish 2 or 3 times. (Mixture firms as it cools.) Let stand for 15 minutes. Refrigerate for at least 8 hours, or overnight.

Lift cheesecake from pan using ends of parchment paper. Peel away parchment and place cheesecake on serving plate. Decorate top with chocolate curls, cherry pie filling or fresh cherries, if desired.

Creamy Orange Chiffon Pie

Crust:

¼ cup plus 1 tablespoon butter
  or margarine
2 teaspoons grated
  orange peel
1⅓ cups finely crushed crisp
  rice cereal crumbs
2 tablespoons sugar

Filling:

4 eggs, separated
⅔ cup orange juice
¾ cup plus 2 tablespoons
  sugar, divided
1 envelope (.25 oz.)
  unflavored gelatin
2 teaspoons grated
  orange peel
⅓ cup half-and-half

6 to 8 servings

Place butter and 2 teaspoons orange peel in 9-inch pie plate. Microwave at High for 1½ to 1¾ minutes, or until butter melts. Stir in remaining crust ingredients. Press mixture firmly against sides and bottom of pie plate. (Pressing with a custard cup works well.) Microwave at High for 1½ to 2 minutes, or until crust is set, rotating plate once. Set aside.

Place 4 egg yolks in medium mixing bowl. Reserve egg whites in large mixing bowl. To egg yolks, add orange juice, ½ cup sugar, the gelatin and orange peel. Mix well. Blend in half-and-half. Microwave at 50% (Medium) for 8 to 14 minutes, or until mixture thickens slightly, stirring with whisk 3 or 4 times. Place bowl in larger bowl containing 1 to 2 inches ice water. Chill both bowls for about 20 minutes, or until mixture is very cold, but not set.

Using electric mixer, beat reserved egg whites until foamy. Gradually add remaining ¼ cup plus 2 tablespoons sugar while continuing to beat until mixture forms stiff peaks. Fold orange mixture into egg white mixture. Pour evenly into crust. Chill for at least 3 hours, or until set. Garnish pie with orange slices or orange zest, if desired.

Quick & Easy Ice Cream Pie

1 quart ice cream (cardboard container)
½ cup chopped nuts
¼ cup liqueur (any complementary flavor)
1 6 oz. (8-inch) ready-to-use graham cracker pie crust

One pie

Open ice cream carton and place directly in microwave oven. Microwave at 50% (Medium) for 30 seconds to 1 minute, or until ice cream softens. Place ice cream in medium mixing bowl. Stir in nuts and liqueur. Spoon filling into graham cracker crust. Freeze for at least 2 hours, or until pie is firm. Garnish with ice cream topping, fresh fruit or whipped topping, if desired.

Pink Piña Colada Pie ▲

2 cups flaked coconut
¼ cup butter or margarine
2 pkgs. (8 oz. each) cream cheese
½ cup cream of coconut
2 egg yolks
1 can (8 oz.) crushed pineapple, drained
3 or 4 drops red food coloring

6 to 8 servings

Spread coconut evenly in bottom of 9-inch pie plate. Microwave at High for 4½ to 6 minutes, or until golden brown, tossing with fork after every minute. Set aside.

In 1-cup measure, microwave butter at High for 1¼ to 1½ minutes, or until melted. Drizzle butter over coconut. Toss to coat. Press coconut mixture against sides and bottom of pie plate. Microwave crust at High for 1 minute. Set aside.

In medium mixing bowl, microwave cream cheese at 50% (Medium) for 3½ to 4½ minutes, or until softened, stirring once. Add remaining ingredients. Beat at medium speed of electric mixer until mixture is smooth. Pour mixture into prepared crust. Microwave at 50% (Medium) for 10 to 12 minutes, or until pie is almost set in center, rotating plate 3 or 4 times. Refrigerate pie for 8 hours or overnight before serving. Garnish with maraschino cherries, if desired.

Creative Crafts

Flower Drying

The microwave oven accelerates the drying of fresh flowers. Simply bury the flowers in a drying agent, like silica gel, microwave briefly and let stand for 12 hours. Silica gel absorbs moisture while supporting the flower in its natural shape. The gel can be reused several times.

Cut flowers in the early morning or late afternoon. Select fresh, dry blossoms that are not fully opened. Avoid flowers that are already in full bloom or have bruised or wilted petals.

Flowers with vivid colors — red, orange, yellow, blue, purple or deep pink — retain their color best. Dark red flowers may appear black when dried; use them in potpourri. Whites and pastels will turn brown.

After drying, spray flowers with hair spray or acrylic spray coating, available at art supply or craft stores. Silica gel, florists' wire and tape are available at craft shops or florists.

Type of flower	Number	Dish size	Silica gel	Microwave at High
Carnations, large	2	1½-quart	6 cups	2 to 3 minutes
Carnations, small	4	1½-quart	6 cups	1½ to 2½ minutes
Chrysanthemums, medium	3	1½-quart	6 cups	2 to 2½ minutes
Daffodils	1	2-cup measure	2 cups	2 to 2½ minutes
Daisies, large	2	1½-quart	4 cups	1½ to 2 minutes
Daisies, small	4	1½-quart	4 cups	1½ to 2 minutes
Roses, miniature	4	1½-quart	6 cups	2 to 2½ minutes
Tulips	1	2-cup measure	2 cups	2½ to 3 minutes

Dried Flowers

What you need:

Flowers (opposite)
Scissors
Silica gel

Small paint brush
Hair spray or acrylic spray
  coating

Florists' wire
Florists' tape
Silk leaves (optional)

How to Microwave Dried Flowers

Trim stems of selected flowers to within ½ inch of flower base. Place one-third of silica gel in dish.

Arrange flowers, blossoms up, in dish. Carefully sprinkle with remaining silica gel, filling spaces between petals and covering flowers completely.

Place dish in microwave. Place ½ cup water in 1-cup measure; set next to dish in oven. Microwave at High, as directed in chart (opposite), or until gel feels very warm, rotating dish once.

Let flowers stand in silica gel for 12 hours to complete drying. Carefully pour off silica, and lift out dried flowers. Shake gently to remove excess gel. Use fine-bristled paintbrush to remove any remaining gel.

Spray flowers with hair spray for protection. Dry flowers completely. Attach florists' wire to stems of the flowers.

Wrap wire with florists' tape. Connect silk leaves to wire stem, if desired, and wrap entire wire with florists' tape.

Dried Flower Wreath ▲

What you need:
Assorted dried flowers
  (page 146)
Baby's breath
Very thin florists' wire
Florists' tape

1 twig wreath (available at craft
  stores)
Hair spray or acrylic spray
  coating
Ribbon (optional)

1 wreath

Attach florists' wire to dried flowers and to small bunches of baby's
breath. Wrap with florists' tape to secure flower to wire. Thread prepared
flowers and baby's breath through wreath, with baby's breath below
flowers. Twist wires together and wrap or weave around back of wreath.
Spray dried flowers with hair spray or acrylic spray. Let dry. Decorate
with ribbon. Hang wreath with wire.

Dried Flower Basket

What you need:
Assorted dried flowers (page 146)
Florists' wire
Florists' tape
Floral foam
Decorative basket
Hair spray or acrylic spray
  coating

Attach wire to stems of dried flowers with florists' tape. Cut floral
foam to fit bottom of decorative
basket. Arrange flowers by insert-
ing taped stems into foam. Spray
dried flowers with hair spray.
Let dry.

Potpourri

What you need:

1 large jar with lid
3 or 4 small decorative jars or containers, with covers

½ cup non-iodized salt
1 tablespoon whole allspice
1 tablespoon whole cloves
1 tablespoon juniper berries
1 tablespoon dried grated orange peel
4 cinnamon sticks, broken up
4 cups dried flower petals (use mostly roses; page 146)
1 bottle (¼ oz.) lavender and rose-scented oil (alternative oils available at craft or drugstores)

In small mixing bowl, combine salt, allspice, cloves, juniper berries, orange peel and cinnamon sticks. Mix well. Set aside. Layer 2 cups flower petals in large jar. Sprinkle with half the lavender and rose oil. Spoon salt mixture over petals. Layer remaining flower petals over salt mixture and sprinkle with remaining oil. Close jar tightly. Shake gently to mix.

Label jar with date. Let potpourri age in covered jar for 4 to 6 weeks, shaking jar once a week. Divide mixture between decorative jars or containers.

Let open jar of potpourri stand for 1 to 2 hours, to scent room as desired. Yields about 2½ cups.

TIPS: Display and store dried flowers by layering loosely in a decorative, see-through jar. Cover jar tightly.

For scented sachet, cut 6-inch squares of thin cotton fabric and place about 2 teaspoons potpourri in center of each. Bring sides up and tie tightly with narrow ribbon, enclosing potpourri. Use to scent closets or drawers.

How to Microwave Aromatic Dough Ornaments

Aromatic Dough Ornaments

What you need:

- Floured board
- Rolling pin
- Cookie cutters
- Whole allspice and cloves
- Small paintbrush
- Garlic press
- Wooden picks
- Drinking straw
- Vegetable cooking spray
- 1 pie plate (10-inch)

Dough:

- 2¾ cups all-purpose flour
- ¾ cup salt
- ¼ cup ground cinnamon
- 1 tablespoon ground allspice
- 1 tablespoon ground cloves
- ¾ teaspoon powdered alum
- 1¼ cups water

Combine flour, salt, cinnamon, allspice, cloves and alum in medium mixing bowl. Mix well. Add water. Mix well to form dough. Shape dough into ball. Knead on lightly floured board for about 5 minutes, or until dough is smooth. (If too stiff, sprinkle with additional water; if too moist, add flour.)

Work with small portions of dough at a time. Roll dough to ¼-inch thickness. Cut out shapes with 2½ to 4-inch cookie cutters. Decorate tops of cut-outs with cloves and allspice, or with bits of dough (moisten dough with water-dipped paint brush and join to cut-out). Store remaining dough in plastic bag.

Push small amounts of dough through garlic press for textured "hair" or "fur" for animal or people shapes, or use a wooden pick to texture surface. Using a drinking straw, cut hole (at least ⅜-inch) near top of cut-out for hanging.

Spray 10-inch pie plate with vegetable cooking spray. Place four 2½ to 3-inch, or three 3½ to 4-inch cut-outs in prepared pie plate. Microwave at 30% (Medium Low) for 5 to 8 minutes, or until tops of cut-outs feel dry, rotating plate and checking ornaments after every 2 minutes.

Remove ornaments to rack and set aside for 24 hours to complete drying. Insert thin ribbon through holes and tie for hanging. If desired, spray decorations lightly with vegetable cooking spray for a glossier appearance.

◄ Spiced Wall Hanging

What you need:

5 aromatic dough ornaments
    (2½-inch; page 151)
5 cinnamon sticks
1 yard ribbon (⅝ to ¾-inch)
    Extra ribbon for bow

              1 wall hanging

From back side of first ornament, thread ribbon through hole and loop over cinnamon stick. Re-thread ribbon back through ornament. Continue threading ribbon through ornaments and looping around cinnamon sticks, leaving about 3 inches between ornaments. On final ornament, leave ribbon hanging 3 or 4 inches below for decoration. Cut bottom of ribbon at an angle or with a decorative notch. Tie extra ribbon in bow and secure at top of wall hanging with needle and thread.

Modeling Clay ►

1 box (16 oz.) baking soda
1 cup cornstarch
1¼ cups cold water
    Food coloring (any color)

In large mixing bowl, combine soda and cornstarch. In 2-cup measure, combine water and food coloring. Pour colored water over soda mixture. Stir until smooth. Microwave at High for 4 to 8 minutes, or until mixture is stiff but can still be stirred, stirring after every minute. Cover clay with damp towel until cool. Knead until smooth. Store clay in airtight containers or plastic bags.

Index